A Summer In The Pyrénées, 2

You are holding a reproduction of an original work that is in the public domain in the United States of America, and possibly other countries. You may freely copy and distribute this work as no entity (individual or corporate) has a copyright on the body of the work. This book may contain prior copyright references, and library stamps (as most of these works were scanned from library copies). These have been scanned and retained as part of the historical artifact.

This book may have occasional imperfections such as missing or blurred pages, poor pictures, errant marks, etc. that were either part of the original artifact, or were introduced by the scanning process. We believe this work is culturally important, and despite the imperfections, have elected to bring it back into print as part of our continuing commitment to the preservation of printed works worldwide. We appreciate your understanding of the imperfections in the preservation process, and hope you enjoy this valuable book.

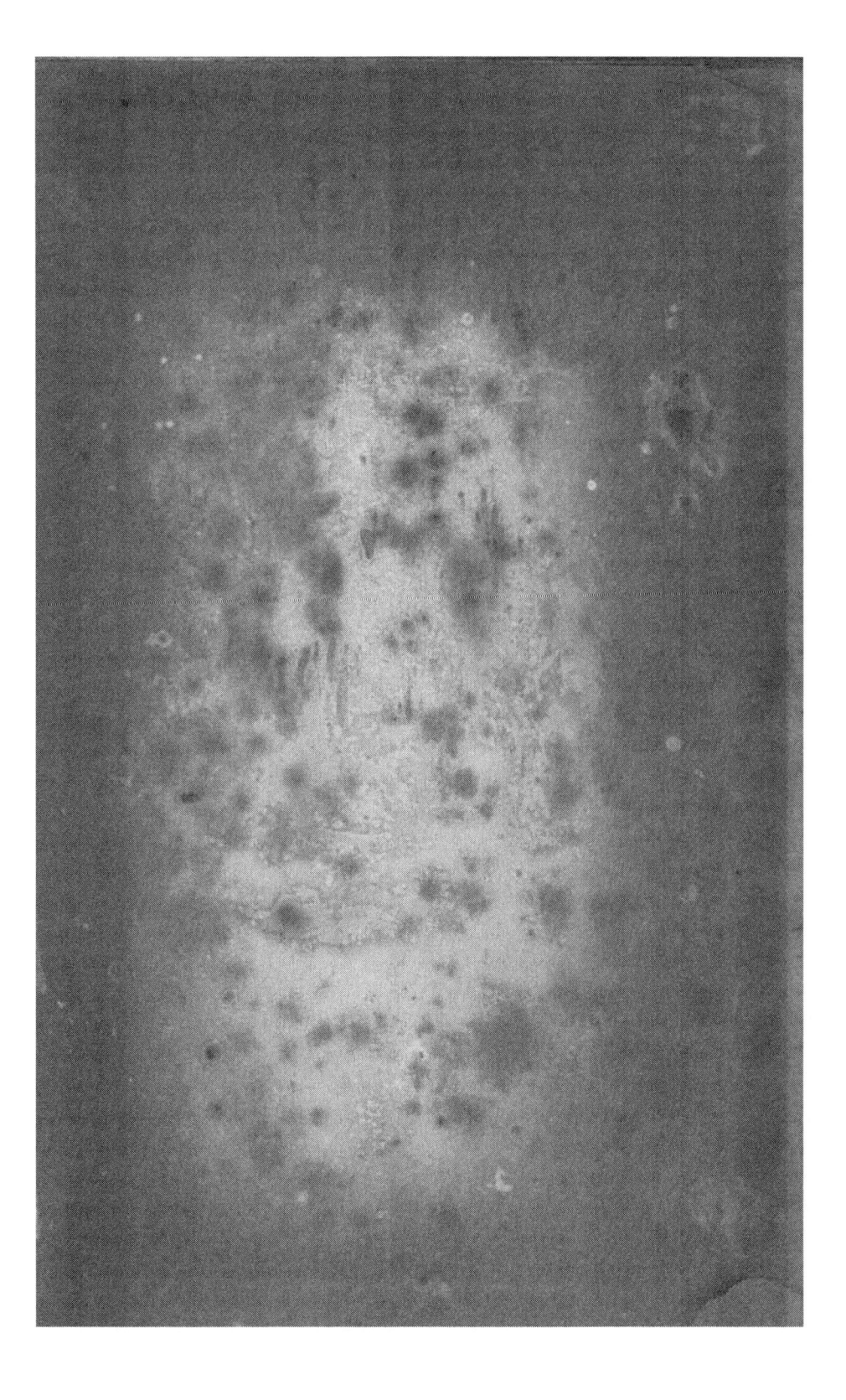

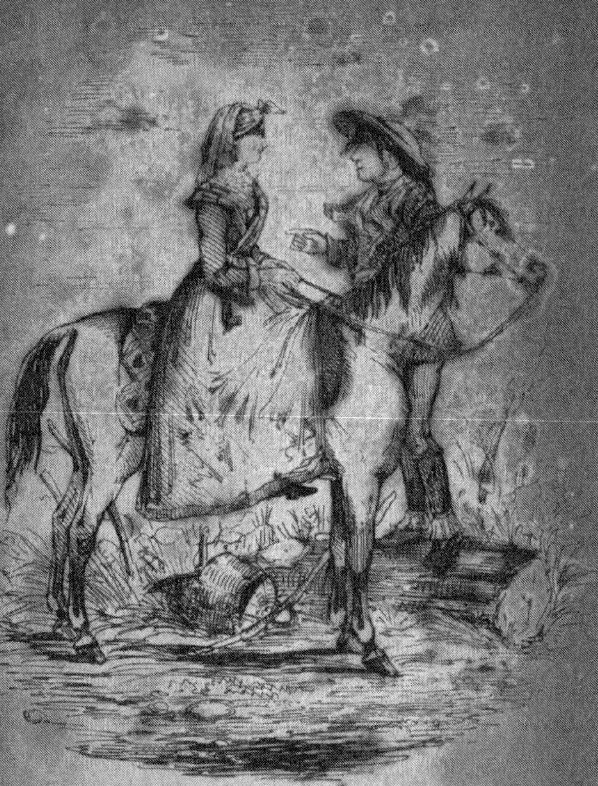

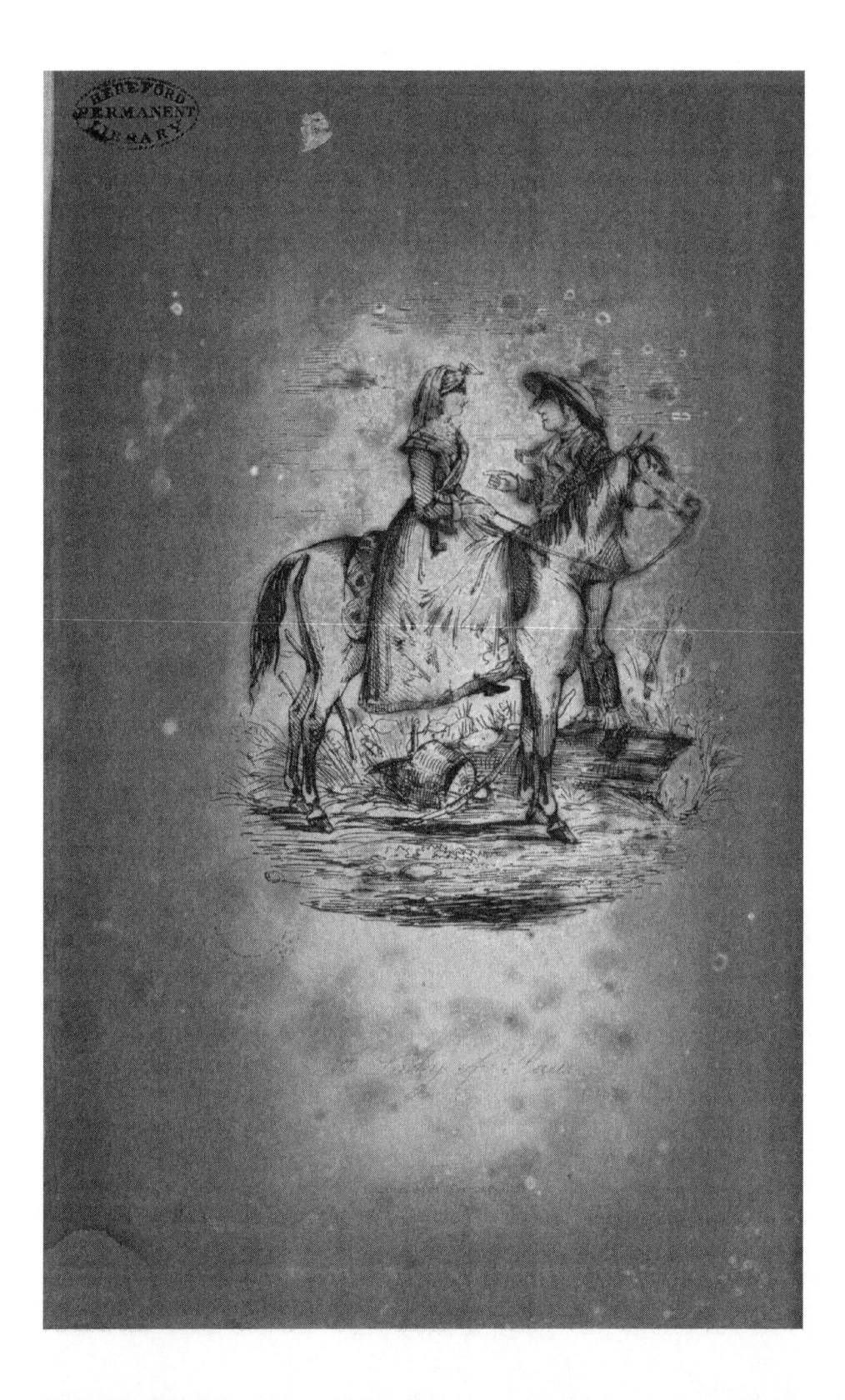

A SUMMER

IN

THE PYRÉNÉES.

BY THE
HON. JAMES ERSKINE MURRAY.

SECOND EDITION.

IN TWO VOLUMES.

VOL. II.

LONDON:
JOHN MACRONE, ST. JAMES'S SQUARE.
M.DCCC.XXXVII.

JOHN HADDON, CASTLE STREET, FINSBURY.

ILLUSTRATIONS TO VOLUME II.

A Lady of Pau . . . (to face title) p. 120
Peasants of the Landes 21
Antoine . . . , . . . 48
Peasants of Bareges 86
Peasant Woman Crossing the Tourmalet . . 90

CONTENTS.

CHAPTER XIV.

Bagnères de Bigorre—Its environs—Little knowledge which the French have of the Pyrénées—Valley of the Campan—St. Marie—French Protestant clergyman—Valley d'Aure—Counts of Armagnac—Path to Luchon—Effects of a dreadful thunder storm—Viel—Destruction of the village of St. Lary—Exquisite valley of Tramesaigues—Force of the Flooded river—Village of Aragnouet—Account of the late awful storm—Plan—Grandeur of the Pyrénean mountains—Port of Cambiel—Mountain dairy 1

CHAPTER XV.

Ramond—Mont Perdu—Valley of the Lavedan—Plan of the ascent of Mont Perdu—Gedre—The famous Peyrada, or Chaos—Devotion of the peasantry—Gavarnie—The Marboré—Its appearance in Winter and in Summer—Ascent to the Breche de Roland—Magnificence of the Breche—Murder of a Spanish muleteer—Descent from the Breche—Spanish side of the Marboré—Mountains in a state of decomposition—Superstitions of the Spanish shepherds—Appearance of Mont Perdu—Pyrénean shepherd's mode of collecting his flocks together—Night in a cave 25

CHAPTER XVI.

Ascent of Mont Perdu—Its difficulties—Herd of izards—Dangerous paths—Summit—A mountain view—Formations of Mont Perdu—Lake of Mont Perdu—Respiration at great altitudes—Descent of the mountain—Change of Weather—Dangerous passage of the Breche de Roland—Difficulty in crossing its glacier—Descent to the Oule of the Marboré—Its cataracts—Disbelief of the Aubergiste of Gedre—Valley of Gavarnie—Pas de L'Echelle—St. Sauveur . 57

CHAPTER XVII.

Basin of Luz—Its great beauty and fertility—Pic de Bergoms—Church of Luz—Baths of St. Sauveur—Castle of St. Marie—Visit of Burke to the Pyrénées—Valley of the Bastan—Village of Bareges, and its mineral springs—Appearance of Bareges in Winter—Curious method of warming themselves adopted by the peasantry—Environs of Bareges—Pic du Midi de Bigorre—Lac d'Oncet—Valleys of Estaubé and Heas—Superstition of the mountaineers—Thunder storm upon the Tourmalet—Gorge of Pierfitte—Its unequalled grandeur—Valley of Argeles—Beauty of its features, and mildness of its climate—Route to Cauteretz—Cauteretz, and its baths—Hunting quarters—Port d'Espagne—Lac de Gaube—Melancholy fate of an English lady and gentleman—Sorrow of the Peasantry at the event—Boiling springs 78

CHAPTER XVIII.

Defile of Lourdes—Castle of Lourdes—Its history interesting to Englishmen—Its gallant defence by Ernault de Bearn—The Chivalry of France driven from before its walls—Assassination of Ernault—Continued defence of Lourdes by his brother—Route from Lourdes to Pau—France pittoresque—St. Pe—Betharram—Pilgrimages to its Calvary—The mingled devotion and hilarity of the peasantry—Plain of Bearn—Chateau of Corraze—Veneration of the Bearnais peasantry for the memory of Henri Quatre—Pau—Its attractions—Splendid view of the mountains—Society of Pau—Its

CONTENTS. vii

Page

origin—Bernadotte, King of Sweden—Climate of Pau—Hanoverian Baron—Anecdote of George the Third and Queen Charlotte—Anecdote of a German soldier 100

CHAPTER XIX.

Pyrénean horses—Their character—Conjectures regarding the race—The Haras—Breeding of horses in the South—The ignorance of the French upon the subject—Expense and inefficiency of the Haras—Cheapness of horses—Great fairs—Horsedealers—Mode of bargaining—Spanish mule dealers—Their fine appearance—Number of mules exported from France into Spain—Price of Mules—String of mules—Extreme honesty of the Spanish mule merchants—Horse-races in the South—Their character—Vanity of the French—Description of a fox-hunt. 133

CHAPTER XX.

Superstitions of the Bearnais, and Haute Pyrénean peasantry—Remnants of ancient mythology—Zeal in celebrating their religious ceremonies—Pilgrimages—Disregard of the Decrees which abolished religion—Character of the inhabitants of Bearn—Ancient Laws of their country—Dislike of the new laws of division—Various superstitions of the mountaineers—Ceremonies at their marriages—Superstitions of the Roussillon peasantry—Celebration of the mysteries—Processions of the Flagellans—Processions of the Semaine Sainte—Poetry and music of the Pyrénées 161

CHAPTER XXI.

Valley of the Neiss—Its great beauty—Source of the Neiss—Valley d'Ossau—Marble pillars in the church of Bielle, and anecdote of Henri IV.—Laruns—Route to Eaux Bonnes—Village of Eaux Bonnes, and mineral springs—Its environs—Hunters of the Valley d'Ossau—Fine appearance and good character of its peasantry—Best period for hunting in the Pyrénées—Izard and bear hunting—Narrow escape of a friend on a hunting excursion—Unsatisfactory pursuit of a bear and cubs—Fonda " le pere des Chasseurs de la Vallée

CONTENTS.

Page

d'Ossau"—Appearance and character of the man—Stalking of an izard—Results—Driving of a herd of izards—Result—Presence of mind of Pyrénean hunters—Numerous herds of isards—Valley of Sousouel—Construction of a hut—Arrival of our provisions—Fonda's adventures, and death-bed scene of his father . . . 191

CHAPTER XXII.

Expedition to Eaux Chaudes in winter—Pass of La Hourat—Its dangerous character—Hotels of the Pyrénées in winter—Scenery in the Valley of the Eaux Chaudes—Entrance to the Forest of Gabas—Village of Gabas—Mode of churning butter—French soldier—General Alava—Feelings of French soldiery towards the Russians—Anecdote of a bear hunter—Forests of the Pyrénées—Magnificent silver firs—Unskilfulness of woodsmen—Effects of the high price of iron in France—Troop of Spaniards—La Cas de Brusette—Blind Spaniard—Cascade—The frontier—Village of Sallient—Posada—Village doctor—Family Scene—Political dispute—Dance—Return to Bearn 223

APPENDIX.

Sketch descriptive of the formation, appearance, and character of the Pyrénées 257
Of the Bearnais Language 290
Specimens of Bearnais Poetry 296
Heights of the most remarkable places in the Pyrénées . . 305
Explanation of certain terms peculiar to the Pyrénées . . 315

A SUMMER IN THE PYRENEES.

CHAPTER XIV.

Bagnères de Bigorre—Its environs—Little knowledge which the French have of the Pyreneés—Valley of the Campan—St. Marie—French Protestant Clergyman—Valley d'Aure—Counts of Armagnac—Path to Luchon—Effects of a dreadful Thunder Storm—Viel—Destruction of the Village of St. Lary—Exquisite Valley of Tramesaigues—Force of the flooded River—Village of Aragnouet—Account of the late awful Storm—Plan—Grandeur of the Pyrenean Mountains—Port of Cambiel—Mountain Dairy.

BAGNERES de Bigorre, the most fashionable of all the Pyrenean watering places, is neither situated in the mountains nor in the plains; the buttresses of the great mountains to the south of it, do indeed stretch out to the right and left of its sweet valley of the Campan, but in character they are soft and gentle, abounding in sunny slopes and shady groves, and just sufficiently imposing to constitute a connecting link between the mountains and the plains.

From the flattering descriptions which various of the Parisien " water drinkers " have given of Bagnères and its environs, it has appeared to them to be " un rendezvous d'amour; le jeune homme caresse du regard les jolies femmes etrangères ou citadines; le moraliste prepare ses tablettes, à l'aspect de cette foule d'originaux de toutes nations; le naturaliste, au milieu des chants de Sybaris, prête l'oreille au murmure lointain des gaves, à la chute des rochers sourcilleux; l'artisan, le parasite, viennent spéculer sur les vices des riches; le joueur s'y montre, n'ayant d'autre instinct que le gôut de l'or, d'autre divinité que le hasard aveugle et cruel : ainsi Bagnères réunit tout ce qui est la honte, la pitié, le charme, et l'honneur de l'humanité. C'est l'abrégé d'une capitale."

It *is* a great city in miniature, and that is the chief reason why Bagnères is not a favourite of mine, at least during its season—August and September, when Luchon, Barèges, St. Sauveur, Cauteretz, the Eaux bonnes, and the Eaux chaudes send forth their quota of visitors, who, to the number of seven or eight thousand, assemble in this little town, to indulge in all the gaieties of the metropolis, and as far as possible get rid of the ennui which every real Parisien supposes must prevail without its barriers.

Bagnères is, however, one of the neatest, and as I have before observed, one of the cleanliest little towns of France. The waters of the Adour circulate among its streets, which are in general more open and airy than those of most southern towns; the houses are in many places detached from each other, and surrounded with pretty gardens, and villas abound in its vicinity. These qualities and attractions would of themselves be sufficient to induce strangers to visit Bagnères; but it has besides various other advantages. It has its mineral waters and sudatory baths, for those who indulge in such abominations; its Frascati establishment for dancing and gaming, and its reading rooms and museums, for those whose health or whose laziness will not permit them to study the exquisite and not far distant book of nature, whose leaves are no where more gorgeously illuminated than in the vicinity of Bagnères, and form collections from its thousand curiosities for themselves. The walks, and rides, and drives which surround Bagnères, which ascend the hills in which it is embosomed, and penetrate into their little valleys and recesses, are many of them exceedingly beautiful, some of them remarkably so.

We are now arrived in the best known and most frequented district of the Pyreneés; I might almost add, the *only* known district of these mountains; scarcely any one—and least of all the French—quitting the beaten track inclosed by the valleys d'Ossau upon the west, and of Luchon on the east. A solitary Englishman now and then strays across these boundaries, and discovers the great beauties which lie beyond them; but these intruders into their solitudes are yet rare; few strangers have hitherto contemplated the magnificent scenery which they contain, and which in a thousand places may be met with, and where the traveller may, as I have done, wander for weeks or months without encountering any human being, excepting the natives. The known district of the Pyreneés, therefore, forms as it were a little island in the centre of the range, and in extent is not more than a fifth part of the whole. But even in this comparatively small district, there are many most picturesque valleys which are seldom visited, either because they are situated apart from the usual paths chosen by the guides, or do not lead from one watering place to another. One of the least known, and most beautiful of these unvisited valleys is that through which I am about to conduct the reader.

Bagnères and the district to the east of it, were already well known to me, and as it was my intention to make the ascent of Mont Perdu ere the weather became so broken as to prevent me, I made a very short stay in that gay little town upon the present occasion, but accompanied by one of my former companions, left Bagnères for Gèdre. The usual route would have been to cross the Tourmalet to Barèges and Luz, and proceed up the valley of Gavarnie; and the guides, if asked, would have declared that there was no other path across the mountains.

More prose and poetry have been lavished in extolling the beauties of the valley Campan than any other spot in Europe. This has been chiefly by French writers, whose ignorance of the surpassing loveliness of hundreds of the other Pyrenean valleys, has led them to suppose that the Campan is the finest of the whole. They have, therefore, selected it simply because they know it, and have bestowed just as much praise upon it as to disappoint those who have expected to find it the paradise which they have portrayed, and to detect their ignorance of the incomparably more exquisite scenery in which their own mountains abound.

The valley Campan has its rich fields, its grassy slopes, its crystal river, its wooded summits, and its shady dells; and with a profusion of such features, it cannot be otherwise than beautiful; in addition, it is a garden of industry and plenty, and cannot, therefore, be otherwise than most pleasing to the beholder, and justly deserves very high encomiums: but that the French, in the prose and poetry which the charms of the Pyreneés have elicited from them, should have fallen into the egregious error of adopting the Campan as the maximum of real or ideal picturesque beauty, establishes beyond a doubt the little knowledge which they have of the Pyreneés.

Accompanied by one of the guides of the place, we left Bagnères at an early hour in the morning, and proceeded up its valley. We soon passed through the little town of Campan, from which the valley takes its name, and where every child which can lisp the words, " Monsieur, voulez vous un bouquet?" presents a rosebud, an asparagus stock, or any thing which may appear as an excuse for beggary; or when taken unawares, and no flower or vegetable is at hand, do not hesitate to substitute, " Monsieur, voulez vous me donner un sous?"

The valley narrows as we approached the village of St. Marie, where the road to Grip branches off from it. This road to Grip is that which is also taken to cross the Tourmalet to Barège, and which I shall have occasion to mention when we arrive at that part of our progress through the Pyreneés. The road after passing St. Marie still continues to wind along the side of the river, and the valley becomes entirely pastoral. The mountains assume a more dignified character, and the Pic d'Arbizon, which towers far above the others, rises in front, the avant guard of the magnificent mountains beyond it.

By the way-side there is a little auberge, called Paillole, near the spot where one of Augustus' generals is said to have defeated the Bigorrians; and thither, accompanied by a stranger whom we had overtaken, we went to feed ourselves and horses. Wine, bread, and cheese, most excellent butter, and delicious milk were presented to us; the simple but wholesome and substantial items of a mountain breakfast. Our new acquaintance we discovered to be a Protestant clergyman from Bayonne, and a most liberal minded and intelligent person, and intimately acquainted with the writings of our Scottish worthies, many of which have been translated into the French language, and are numbered among the " standard works " of the French Protestant family libraries.

After breakfast, we proceeded on our journey, and our new acquaintance went to Bagnères. At a short distance from Paillole, we entered the extensive pine forests which hang upon the ridge of mountain which separates the upper districts of the Adour from the valley d'Aure. The ascent of the ridge is lengthy but gradual, and from the Hourquette d'Aure the view of the valley beneath is very fine. It is a bird's-eye view of a rich and expansive valley, diversified with verdant meadows, and fields of yellow grain. Towns and villages crown its most defensible positions, and dark forests clothe the sterility of many of its surrounding heights. This ridge which separates the Adour from the Garonne, is the most remarkable of the Pyreneés. No other is equal to it in length, or so unbroken in its course. It extends from the central range of the mountains, beginning a short distance to the east of Mont Perdu; separates the valleys Campan and d'Aure, forcing the rivers of these valleys to take the opposite courses; stretches away by Mielan through the departments of the Gers and Landes, and separates the Medoc country from the sandy plains of the coast, among which it terminates at the little village of Vendais.

The Counts of Armagnac were the ancient lords of the valley d'Aure, and at Arreau and Bordères are the ruins of their castles. The restless ambition which characterized the various members of the Armagnac family, is apparent in history; their feuds with their neighbours the Counts of Foix, and their rebellions against their sovereigns often deluging the country with blood, and plunging it into all the miseries of civil war. The last unfortunate of the race was John the Fifth, less famous for his revolt against Charles the Seventh, than his love for his sister Isabella, whom he married in defiance of the threatened maledictions of the Papal court. The consequences of this crime were his banishment, and the forfeiture of his estates, which were, however, upon his making peace with the court of Rome, and separating from his sister-wife, restored to him by Louis XI. But he again revolted, and was assassinated when about to surrender after a gallant defence of his capital. The family became extinct, his friends and supporters were executed, and his dominions finally annexed to the crown of France.

Prior to the acquisition of this territory by the family of Armagnac, Pierre, Count of Bigorre, gave Bordères to the Templers, who erected it into a Commanderie, which it continued until the massacre of the knights in 1313, and the destruction of their order; when all the knights of Bigorre, with their commander, Bernard de Montagu, were executed at Auch, and their lands and castles bestowed upon the Commanderie of St. John of Jerusalem, at Aureilhan, near Tarbes.

The path which through the valley d'Aure conducts to Luchon, passes by Arreau, then enters the valley de Louron, and crossing by the Port de Peyresourbe into the valley Larbous, unites with the path which we have already described when visiting the lake of Seculejo from Luchon. We did not descend into the valley of Aure by the usual path from the Hourquette, but skirted along the summit of the ridge until we came directly above the village of Ancizin, where the route being no longer practicable for horses, we were obliged to leave the heights, and scramble down the abrupt steeps above that village.

The valley is rich and fertile, producing all kinds of grain, but the upper parts of it had suffered very severely by the most awful thunderstorm which, in the memory of the inhabitants, had ever happened in this district. Thunderstorms are in general of short duration; but this storm, which had caused so much injury in the valley, raged not only for days but weeks. Towards Viel the first appearance of its desolating effects presented themselves. The road, hitherto broad and tolerably good, was lost among fields of sand and gravel, which the river, flooded by the immensity of rain which fell, had swept from the upland districts, and poured over the most fertile soils of the valley, overwhelming them in ruin.

The sad aspect of the scene was greatly enhanced by the solitary patches of productive land which, saved by the currents being turned aside by a hedgerow or clump of trees, yielded its wonted returns, surrounded by barrenness and sterility. But the destruction of a part of the valley before arriving at the considerable village of Viel, was comparatively trifling to that which we were to witness some distance beyond it.

The valley begins to contract above Viel, the path winding no longer in the plain, and ascends the mountain-side ere it enters the gorge of St. Lary.

Here it was that the late storm had wrought the greatest destruction. The village of St. Lary, situated in the centre of its beautiful basin, surrounded by fertile fields and rich meadows, of which each family had its own little portion, was one of the most contented and happy in the whole district, until this fearful storm took place. The swollen river, whose channel through the upper parts of the valley had become nearly choked up by immense quantities of débris, and the enormous rocks which each mountain stream, nourished by the rains into a mighty torrent, had swept from the steeps, and torn from precipices, having at last acquired sufficient force to overcome all the barriers which obstructed its progress through the contracted defiles of Plan and Aragnouet, dashing into its resistless flood the natural bulwarks which for ages had stemmed its most rebellious currents, burst from the gorge of St. Lary, and, teeming with the spoils of its destructive course, spread its abundant harvest over the defenceless valley. The first burst of its pent up wrath was wreaked upon the commune of St. Lary. The inhabitants were driven from their village, the greater part of which was buried beneath the ruins of the upper valleys, and their smiling fields, their verdant meadows, their little all was by this fell swoop of desolation for ever lost to them.

The Moors of Spain, the soldiers of Augustus, the destroyers of the Armagnacs, had ravaged the valley, and shed the blood of its inhabitants, but over each and all of these calamities time had spread its healing influence, and repaired the mischiefs; not so will it be with this visitation; the sufferers have, indeed, no slain friends or relatives to weep for, but they have starving families who call in vain to them for bread. Industry can never restore to them the soil which had hitherto supplied their simple wants, and the vista of time can present to them no period at which their children may, in smiling plenty, again assemble in the "hamlet fane" of their forefathers.

The path high above the river, hung upon the mountain-side, and is in many places very narrow. At one of these awkward spots we encountered a string of mules laden with wool. It was impossible to pass them, and as neither party could turn round, we dismounted and backed our horses to a wider part of the path, where the mules could pass us; but even there it was so narrow, that the panniers of one of the mules having caught in the flap of my saddle, the concussion, slight as it was, nearly threw the animal over the precipice.

The defile which succeeds the gorge of St. Lary, is several miles in length, and does not widen until after the lateral valley of Rioumajou has united with it, when it again entirely alters in character. The valley, which had hitherto been stretching away directly south, bends abruptly to the west, and the traveller can hardly conceive a more exquisite scene than that which the turn in the path unfolded to us. The river still continues to wind close under the path, and the high mountains which lie between the Peak of Arrouye and the Pic Long to tower above it; but the mountains to the south have receded from its banks, and given space for the upland valley of Tramesaigues.

In no other valley of the Pyreneés is that union of beauty, picturesqueness, and sublimity, which is more or less characteristic of the scenery of these mountains, found in such exquisite perfection, and so combined and interwoven together. Fertile fields, upon which the corn still waved, were diversified with rich pastures, and interspersed with varieties of trees, whose foliage was already tinted by the autumnal frosts; the village, occupying a distant nook, was almost hidden amongst the woods which surrounded it; the massy ruins of its castle crowned some cliffs above it. Dark forests clung upon the steep mountains which inclosed the valley, and clothed the numerous gorges and ravines leading to the central range, whose snow-clad summits, and rocky peaks, rising majestically above the whole, formed the back ground of this little fairy land.

Most fortunately for the safety of this beautiful little valley during the late storm, it was situated considerably above the level of the river; so that, excepting where the torrents of its gorges had overflowed their banks, it had escaped unharmed. At its upper end, the mountains on both sides of the river almost touch each other; and the path, crossing to the opposite bank, and scooped out of the rock, leaves the valley through an ancient portal, in which the ponderous gate no longer swung, which, when closed, must have effectually prevented intrusion upon this quarter.

Shortly after passing this portal, we arrived at a place where the tremendous power of the river, when in flood, was fearfully perceptible. Precipices of solid rock inclosed it upon both sides, excepting at one spot, where huge blocks of rock, piled above each other since some convulsion had rent them from the mountains, had for ages stemmed its currents. Situated at a bend of the river, these natural bulwarks, a thousand times stronger than any which the hands of man could raise, were still unable to resist the force of the stream. The foundations of the enormous mass were driven out, and its mountains of rocks precipitated into the bed of the river. The fallen mass had completely choked up the waters until they had so accumulated as to break down the barrier which their own violence had occasioned, and to sweep its ponderous materials before them. The bed of the river had become a perfect chaos of rocks, which in some places formed arches across it, while in others, the stream, losing itself among them, was hidden from our sight; and the path, which by this catastrophe had been entirely destroyed, now wound among the fallen heaps. There was still some danger in passing the spot, as the slightest shower was sufficient to dislodge the rocks which protruded from the exposed side of the mountain, and hurl them into the river.

We proposed remaining all night in the village of Aragnouet, and many scenes of devastation were passed through ere we arrived at it. This village was built, and the district colonized, by the Christians who, towards the end of the seventh century, were expelled from Spain by the Moors.

From the owner of its auberge, we learnt the particulars of the storm which had done so much damage in the valley. Thunder-storms are frequent in the Pyreneés, especially in the vicinity of the central and highest range of the mountains; where, although they are, in general, most common during the spring and autumn, yet few weeks throughout the year pass over in which they have not taken place. Their duration is so seldom beyond the third or fourth day from their commencement, that the peasants look forward to their termination at the end of that period with such confidence as to form their plans, and make their arrangements, as if the circumstance was a certainty; and, should they chance to endure for a week, they regard this prolongation as an extraordinary incident.

The late storm came on towards the end of the spring; and, though it raged with unwonted violence, it was, for the first three or four days, almost disregarded. The peasantry, believing that a limited period was assigned for this warring of the elements, never thought of the sufferings to which they would be subjected should the period be unusually lengthened. Accordingly, they adopted no precautionary measures; they collected no provisions; they did not conceive it necessary to withdraw the shepherds and their flocks from the mountains; and they felt no uneasiness as to their safety.

The fourth day passed, then the week; and still there was no abatement in the violence of the storm. "You can form no idea of its awfulness," said our informer—" it seemed as if the mountains which surround our valley were fighting with each other, and their weapons the thunders and the lightnings. The incessant peals, hurled from one summit to another, rolled back again with more stunning crashings; the lightnings played around our cottages, and during the darkness of the nights, illuminated the mountain-tops, whose fantastic-looking peaks every instant appeared shrouded in a blaze of light; while the rain descended in torrents which no cottage roof could resist, and which threatened to sweep our dwellings from their foundations, and wash us into the river, whose swollen waters, rising far above the limits of their highest floods, were already robbing us of our property. Our thoughts were at first directed to the danger of the shepherds and their flocks, but to whom it was impossible to render assistance; the strongest man among us could not have braved the hurricane for an hour; so we were obliged to leave them to their fate, and bethink us of our own.

"Weeks succeeded weeks, and still the terrible scene was the same. There was no abatement in the thunderings, no interval in the lightnings, nor cessations in the rains. We gave ourselves up for lost, and believed that 'the end of all things was at hand.' It became apparent, that death by famine, or perishing in the waters which raged around us, was the fate which shortly awaited upon all of us. Silent stupified

Peasants of the Landes

London, John Murray, 1837

sorrow overwhelmed us, and our feelings were fast drying up; when, in the end of the sixth week, peace again reigned in the valley, and the clouds cleared away. The change which the first knowledge of the fact wrought upon our despairing minds may be conceived, but cannot be described."

The effects of the storm were dreadful to these poor mountaineers. The shepherds, indeed, had outlived it, but the greater part of their cattle and sheep had perished; and many prosperous years will not make up to them the losses which have befallen them.

We left Aragnouet early next morning, taking along with us one of its inhabitants to conduct us across the high mountains which separate the head of the valley of Arreau from that of Gavarnie, or the Lavedan: the guide whom we had brought from Bagnères, although a native of that town, and been employed for twenty years in his present capacity, had never travelled the route which we had chosen.

Passing the little hamlet of Plan, from which there is a path into the Spanish valleys of Bielsa and Gistain, by the Port de Bielsa, we commenced the ascent of the mountains. The view of the summits of the central range from many parts of the ascent is magnificent. From the Pic de Cambiel, on the west, to the Maladetta, on the east, a crescent of peaks, of every variety of shape and appearance, presented themselves, including the very highest of the Pyreneés, and the most numerous concentrated assemblage of elevated summits in Europe. Higher mountains there are, by a couple of thousand feet, in Switzerland, than are to be found in the Pyreneés; but they are neither numerous, nor situated together. Thus in the district in Switzerland which contains the greatest number of high summits,—the Oberland Bernois,—six mountains, ranging from ten to twelve thousand feet in height, are to be found; whilst, in a similar extent of Pyrenean scenery, twenty-one mountains, varying from ten to eleven thousand feet in height, may be seen and counted from various points of the department in which we now were. The Swiss scenery may be called an *aristocracy* of mountains—the Pyrenean, a *republic;* in the former, a few isolated summits domineer far above the others; in the latter, they are more upon an equality.

The Port of Cambiel, at an elevation of nearly eight thousand feet, is an immense gap between the mountain of the same name, and the outer ridge of the Pic Long. Excepting the Port d'Oo, at the head of the valley Lasto, this port is the highest in the Pyreneés which is passable for horses; and, although very steep towards the summit, yet there is none other which can be passed with less danger.

From the west side of the port, the most striking object to be seen is the Vignemale, whose double cones, but a few feet inferior in height to Mont Perdu, rise above the other summits, and are separated from each other by its enormous glacier, upon whose surface the mid-day sun was shining resplendently. The valley which we now descended, surrounded on all sides by very high mountains, yields the most luxuriant pasturage, and was filled with flocks and herds. The only individual in charge of the first troop which we met was a peasant-girl, who treated us with great civility. Upon my asking if she could give us any milk, she conducted us a little way down the mountain, until we arrived at a spot where a few flags of stone were lying. One of these she raised, and disclosed a little fountain, in which the pitchers containing the produce of her flocks were immersed. Of the contents, deliciously cooled in this little dairy, and given to us with no sparing hand, we drank most liberally; and, shortly after, passing through the meadows above the village of Gedre, where its inhabitants were busily employed in making hay, we arrived at our journey's end.

CHAPTER XV.

Ramond—Mont Perdu—Valley of the Lavedan—Plan of the ascent of Mont Perdu—Gèdre—The Famous Peyrada, or Chaos—Devotion of the Peasantry—Gavarnie—The Marboré—Its appearance in Winter, and in Summer—Ascent to the Breche de Roland—Magnificence of the Breche—Murder of a Spanish Muleteer—Descent from the Breche—Spanish side of the Marboré—Mountains in a state of Decomposition—Superstitions of the Spanish Shepherds—Appearance of Mont Perdu—Pyrenean Shepherd's Mode of collecting his Flocks together—Night in a Cave.

RAMOND, whose name is so intimately connected with the scenery of the Hautes Pyreneés, and whose geological researches among the mountains of that department have tended so greatly to benefit his favourite science, was the first individual who succeeded in attaining the summit of Mont Perdu.

Doubts as to the character of its formations led him to undertake the enterprize, considered most hazardous if not impracticable by the natives of the district. Ramond's first attempts were made upon the northern, or French side of the mountain, over the eternal snows and glaciers which clothe it from its summits to the lake beneath it. The obstacles, however, to the ascent upon that quarter were altogether insurmountable, and the idea of overcoming them was abandoned. Undeterred, however, by these failures, Ramond, several years after the period of his first attempts, stormed the mountain from the Spanish side, and arrived at its summit. The reward of his success was the gratification of ascertaining the fact that this, the second of the Pyreneés, consisted of the formations which he had supposed it to be, thus establishing opinions which he had expressed regarding the structure of this part of the Pyreneés. For his success in the ascent of Mont Perdu, Ramond was greatly, indeed wholly, indebted to the activity and intelligence of a native of Gèdre, by name Rondo.

' Since Ramond led the way, several individuals have ascended Mont Perdu, and I, ambitious to be among the number, resolved to do so likewise. Both Ramond and his friend Rondo have long since been gathered to their fathers; but the latter has bequeathed to his son the honourable, and not altogether barren inheritance of his knowledge of the secret paths of the mountain; and he now enjoys the undisputed privilege of conducting strangers to its summit.

When passing through Gèdre in the winter, I called upon Rondo *the second*, and made the appointment to accompany him to the summit of Mont Perdu, which I had now come to fulfil. Immediately on our arrival in Gèdre, I sent for Rondo, who, as the season for such an expedition was almost terminated, had given up hopes of seeing me; and our plans for the expedition of the ensuing day were soon completed.

The Lavedan, in which we have arrived, comprizes not only the great valley which, commencing beneath the walls of the Marboré, opens into the rich plains of Bearn near the famous college of Betharam, but the whole of the smaller valleys which diverge from the banks of its river, the Gave de Pau, among which are included the valleys of Cauteretz, the Bastan, Heas, and others. The summer and the winter aspects of the Levedan and its dependent valleys, excepting that district of it which extends from the basin of Luz to the circle of the Marboré, and which is very frequently styled the valley of Gavarnie, were already familiar to me. The valley of Gavarnie I had only contemplated during the depths of winter, when its banks, and rocks, and summits, divested of animal and vegetable life, were sheeted in snow and ice, when its villages were almost deserted, and the stillness of its deep gorges and defiles was only broken by the cracking of the ice, or the falling of the avalanche.

Rondo, accompanied by his nephew, who had once made the ascent of Mont Perdu, awoke me by daybreak the next morning, for it was very necessary that we should commence the long and difficult journey which we had before us, at an early hour. The plan of our expedition was to pass the summits of the Marboré by the Breche de Roland, and descending into the valley beyond them, reach before night the base of Mont Perdu;

where, if the Spanish shepherds had not already quitted the high pastures of the Millaris, we should find shelter during the night in their hut; or supposing that the late storms had forced them to descend, we were, in that case, to content ourselves with the most convenient resting place we could find; and bivouack under the shelter of a projecting cliff; or to leeward of a mass of rock; and with the appearance of the first streak of daylight, commence the ascent.

The weather, which for several weeks had been broken and uncertain, had now become apparently settled, and seeming likely to continue so, we did not burden ourselves with a greater stock of provisions than was necessary for two or three days; indeed I hoped to return to Gèdre the following night, should no unforeseen accident befall any of the party. My host of the inn, however, assured me of the impossibility of performing this feat, which, if I had not felt inclined to disbelieve the statements of those who had retreated before the dangers of the ascent to the Breche de Roland, as to their fearful character; and learned to reduce within the limits of *plain* English the *superlatives* with which, upon the most trivial occasions, the French interlard their expressions, and so lavishly make use of in their descriptions, I should scarcely have hinted at performing.

The village of Gèdre is situated in one of those spots so frequently met with in the Pyreneés, where industry and cultivation are found, like an oasis in the desert, embosomed among stern and rocky scenery. The mountains, less abrupt and precipitous than in other parts of the valley, and receding from the banks of the Gave, have permitted the soil of the upper districts to accumulate around their base; and scattered among the natural and artificial terraces, each one of which is the property of a separate individual or family, are the cottages of the peasantry, some of them whitewashed, and all surrounded by little fields of grain, or meadows, whose scanty produce is sufficient to secure their owners from starvation during the winter, and supply their few and simple wants.

The valley again contracts soon after leaving Gèdre, resumes its wild and savage character, and we shortly arrive at the Peyrada or Chaos, where even *desolation* in ruins may be beheld. Some terrible convulsion of nature, acting with awful force upon the great mountains which flank the valley, has torn and rent them in a thousand places, and shivered their granitic summits into pieces. The fallen masses, piled high above each other, and of enormous size, choke up the valley from side to side. Single fragments form arches across the torrent; others, obstructing its progress, force it into rapids or cataracts; and the path, lost in this labyrinth of huge blocks, —such as the Titans may have hurled against the heavens,—winds for a long way among these confused heaps. One of these rocks, held in great veneration by the peasantry of the district, and nearly equal in sanctity to the famous Caillou de l'Araye, in the valley of Heas, is that which is the largest and most remarkable of the millions of the Peyrada. It is called the Raille, or Stone of Notre Dame; and pilgrims to the chapels of Heas or Gavarnie, generally offer their prayers at the bottom of the gigantic mass, or at the top, if their faith gives them courage to climb it.

As we approached Gavarnie, the gloomy solitude of the defile through which we passed, the amazing height of its walls, and the rushing of its Gave, began to lose their interest; and every turn and rising of the path is eagerly passed and topped, in expectation of beholding the great object of astonishment and wonder to the thousands who yearly pass through the valley of Gavarnie to behold it—the magnificent and unequalled scenery of the Marboré. The towers of this immense barrier between the two countries appear in succession; then the glaciers at their base, forming the covering of the perpendicular wall from which they spring; and, lastly, the wall of rock, which, in the form of a crescent, terminates the valley of the Lavedan. The valley again widens near the village of Gavarnie, and the high valley d'Ossone branches away to the right, through which a glimpse of the snow-capped Vignemale may be caught, before crossing the bridge over the Gave.

At the little inn of Gavarnie, where, in the height of the season, the numerous visitors of the scenes in its vicinity rendezvous to partake of the luxuries of its well-managed cuisine, we breakfasted, completed the arrangements for our expedition, and were soon again on our way to the foot of the Marboré. An hour's walk through the meadows which intervene between the village and the Marboré, brought us beneath its gigantic heights. Some idea I may convey to the reader of this extraordinary scene, some faint conception of its sublime grandeur and surpassing magnificence; but to describe the Marboré in that manner which they who have looked upon its wonders must feel that it is entitled to, would be a hopeless task for any pen unguided by the hand of a Milton or a Dante.

This was a second time that I had beheld the Marboré. My first visit to it was in winter, and its appearance then I shall first describe. The plain of Gavarnie, and the Oule, or basin of the Marboré, were covered with snow, many feet in depth, which we crossed with little difficulty. We then found ourselves in the centre of an amphitheatre, whose walls, rising perpendicularly for more than fifteen hundred feet, were draped, in some places from top to bottom, in others midway down, with curtains of polished ice, projecting portions of the dark rock alone marking its transparent surface. Above the circling ramparts of this amphitheatre, and rising from the beds of virgin snow which, crowning their summits, formed a coping worthy of their character, appeared a mountain of terraces, each story dimly outlined by the border of black precipice which supported it; and, from the highest of these terraces, and more than two thousand feet above the ramparts from which they spring, again rise detached columns of solid rock a thousand feet above the pedestal upon which they rest—their capitals, the snows and glaciers which never leave them.

The many cataracts which, at other seasons, dash from the ramparts into the basin beneath, and whose sounding falls ring among the precipices, were now dead; weeks of severe frost had almost dried them up, and the small remnants of their waters trickled down the rocks, and over their icy coatings, noiseless and unobservable. Not a speck of cloud floated in the air, and the sun, beating full upon the glacier above, and the wastes of snow beneath, illuminated their surface with a dazzling brightness.

Such is a faint description of the winter garb worn by the Marboré; one of nature's grandest works; the contemplation of which strikes the beholder with awe and admiration, where—

> "We feel the present Deity, and taste
> The joy of God, to see his awful works;"

and in comparison with which the noblest efforts of man's genius, the gorgeous ruins of antiquity, the Palmyras, and the Coliseums, nay, even the Pyramids, dwindle into insignificance.

The scene was now changed. The summer's burning suns had breathed over the amphitheatre, and the icy curtains of its walls had fallen away. The glacier cushions of its stories had shrunk to half their former size; the fountains of its cataracts were opened up, and a circle of torrents shooting from the stupendous heights, some dashing upon the projecting precipices ere they reached the basin below, were split into slender jets, which a passing gust of wind converted into a shower; others, of greater force, and with more collected waters, were seen, bounding from the platform of the terraces, and, clearing every obstacle, descending unbroken in their fall, until they thundered among the rocks of the Oule. The most magnificent of these cataracts is the origin of the

Gave de Pau. No other cataract in Europe is equal to it in height; and no other portion of European scenery can be compared to that which surrounds its birth-place *.

I left my friend (who was to await my return at Gèdre, or Luz) contemplating the majesty of the Marboré, and proceeded on my route to Mont Perdu.

Advancing until we were nearly opposite to the great cascade, we then turned to the right; and, after crossing the various streams which rush through the upper part of the Oule, we arrived at the spot where a narrow sloping shelf on the side wall of the amphitheatre renders the escalade of the first, and apparently most impracticable part of the ascent, a matter of trifling moment to any one accustomed to step along the

* Je n'ai rien vu dans les Alpes qui resemblât parfaitement à nos Oules, parce que les Alpes n'ont rien qui ressemble à la chaîne du Mont Perdu. L'Oule de Gavarnie, surtout, est un de ces objets singuliers qu' on chercherait en vain hors des Pyreneés : je ne pourrais en donner quelqu' idée aux habitans de la Suisse, qu'en la comparant au petit bassin de Leuck, ou la Gemmi surmontée de ses tours, représenterait le Marboré, moins ses cascades et ses glaciers; encore cette légère analogie ne soutiendrait guére plus les regards du peintre que ceux du géologue.—*Ramond— Voyage au Mont Perdu.*

edge of precipices; and where the track, bending round an angle of the rock, or projecting crag, hangs over the abyss, there the wary contrabandiers, who have trod the path for centuries, have scooped out footsteps, and obviated the difficulties of the passage. In an hour we had surmounted this natural ladder, and entered upon the high pastures called Les Serrades; where, for a few weeks of the year, the Spanish shepherds bring their flocks to feed upon the scanty herbage of the steep acclivities of which they are composed*.

Here, for a moment, we turned to gaze upon the Marboré, whose lofty towers were becoming more distinct and imposing as the objects at their base were dwindling in "dizziness of distance;" and again resumed our march through a succession of small ravines and gorges, confused with masses of rock, and wreaths of snow, until we came to the foot of the great glacier, which extends from the Taillon, the western horn of the crescent, all along the ridge of the Marboré, passing under the Breche de Roland, covering

* The Spanish shepherds rent their pastures from the Commune of Gavarnie.

the terraces of the amphitheatre, and whose detached masses finally unite with the larger one of Mont Perdu.

Turning the western flank of the glacier, we scrambled over a height of loose débris—the least dangerous, but most annoying part of the ascent, the rolling heaps often carrying us along with them, and cheating us of the progress we had made: and, from its summit, crossed the glacier, in an angular direction, towards the Breche. The glacier, though suspended on a very steep acclivity, was passed without any difficulty. A late fall of snow had crusted its otherwise polished surface with a thin coating, which, yielding to our pressure, gave us a perfect security of footing, and I esteemed as incumbrances the provision of iron cramps and poles with which Rondo was provided.

We then stepped upon a narrow plain of snow, in which, towards the Breche, the sun's rays, beating through the immense gap, had formed so deep a hollow as obliged us to make a circuit round it, and pass close under the rocks on the farther side, ere we could gain the famous Breche which the warlike nephew of Charlemagne,—the hero of many a romantic story and tale,—is said, in tradition, to have cleft with his terrible sword in the wall of rock, which, dividing Spain from France, shielded the Moors from the exterminating vengeance of his armies.

Having satisfied my curiosity in gazing from the southern side of the Breche over the mountains and valleys of Arragon, I returned again to the esplanade of snow on the French side, to rivet upon my memory the appearance of this gigantic door-way from that quarter. Let the reader imagine a wall of rock, from three to seven hundred feet high, raised between France and Spain, and actually separating them. Let him then suppose that Roland, mounted on his war-horse, and anxious to pass the barrier, has cut, near the centre, with a stroke of his sword, a breach three hundred feet in width, and he will then have an idea of what the mountaineers have called the Breche de Roland.

The wall is not thick, but derives support from the towers of the Marboré, which rise majestically above its gate, and all its avenues, resembling a citadel such as Roland would have placed there to defend the passage. The battering of the storms and rains, and the atmospheric changes, have left such evidences of their wasting effects upon its surface, especially upon its southern side, as to foretel, in the course of time, the decay of this enormous barrier. The elements have wrought the greatest havoc upon the lower parts of the wall, where it is in a manner excavated, and rendered so top-heavy, that a far slighter convulsion than that which split the Coumelie, and created the Peyrada, would be sufficient to destroy the symmetry of the Marboré, and hurl its lofty towers from their high resting-place into the valleys.

Upon the southern side of the Breche, and at a little distance from it, is a small cavity under its walls, which the contrabandiers use as a place of refuge from the storms, and thither we proceeded to partake of our provisions. It was in this rude chamber that the body of an unfortunate Spaniard, who had been murdered about a fortnight before I visited the place, was found. He had come to the annual fair of Gavarnie, for the purpose of purchasing mules; but, not finding any to his liking, had set off on his return home. Some of his countrymen, aware that he had not parted with the money which he had brought to pay for the mules had he bought them, resolved to murder him, and gain possession of it. He was seen to leave Gavarnie towards the afternoon, with two other Spaniards, who were not known to the villagers, but who seemed to be known to him. A couple of days after the fair, a party left Gavarnie to visit the Breche, one of whom, upon entering the cavity in which we were, observed the arm of a human being protruding from under the stones with which its floor is covered. The alarm was given, and the rest of the party arriving, the body was removed from beneath the heaps which had been piled above it, and recognized by the guides as that of the Spanish muleteer who had left Gavarnie two days before.

Upon the return of the party to Gavarnie, information was given to the authorities of the murder; but they could adopt no measures, either with a view to discover the perpetrators of the crime, or for the burial of the body. The French jurisdiction did not extend a single foot beyond the southern side of the Breche de Roland; a murder committed there was the same as if it had been committed at Madrid; and all that they could do, was to give notice to the nearest Spanish authorities of the circumstance. This they did; and, as the murdered person was a native of one of the neighbouring valleys, his family were soon informed of the event; and his sons, accompanied by their friends, came to the Breche, and carried home his body.

His murderers must have formed their plans before leaving Gavarnie, and fixed upon this spot for the scene of their savage purpose. Here they had come (as is the custom with those who are benighted in crossing the Marboré) to pass the few hours of darkness, before descending the rugged steeps of the Spanish mountains. The murdered man was remarkable for his strength and activity, and quite equal to repel the assaults of any two individuals who attacked him openly; his death must, therefore, have been compassed by the foulest means. Most probably, the muleteer, wholly unconscious of his danger, had fallen asleep, and the murderers, watching for the opportunity, had sheathed their knives in his breast, ere he could be aware of their intentions. Supposing this to have been the case, the strong man, even in his dying moments, must have struggled fiercely with his murderers; for the whole interior of the cavity, the floor and the rocky sides, were still covered and spattered with clotted blood. Never was a crime of deepest dye committed in a situation which yielded more temporal security to its perpetrators, less hope of succour to its victim; where no eye but an Almighty one could rest upon the scene; and where no human ear could hear the wailing cries of the perishing, nor arm be stretched forth to save him.

The body of the murdered was indeed gone; but the traces of the crime were too fresh and recent to permit of us converting the chamber into a salle-à-manger; an unshaded block outside was preferred, and we soon finished our repast.

The view around the French side of the Breche is one of mingled rocks, precipices, snows, and glaciers. On the Spanish side there is no glacier, and scarcely any snow, excepting in the deep crevices which extend along the basis of the Marboré, while the eye can, here and there, discover solitary patches of vegetation among the great rocks, scattered in every direction, and the stony hills heaped one above another.

The usual descent from the Brèche is by a path leading along the ridge for some distance to the right, and which, evading the slopes of débris which lie immediately beneath it, winds down the mountain where its surface is of a more solid nature; but, as following this track would have caused us to make a considerable detour, we chose to go straight down the slopes of débris; where, in reality, there was little danger to be apprehended, provided we did not follow each other, but went down abreast; so that the loosened stones might not, in rolling, strike any of the party. Sometimes walking, sometimes carried along with the slipping mass, we arrived unharmed at the bottom, with our shoes well-filled with sand and pebbles. To have ascended these slopes would have been a very different task; we should then have been in the situation of the poor fellows in the tread-mill, taking many steps, but making little advance.

We then crossed the bottom of this deep ravine, and skirted along the crumbling sides of the Marboré by a scarcely perceptible path, a single false step upon which would have given us a roll of many hundred feet, until we reached the Millaris,—the name of the narrow plain which stretches towards Mont Perdu, and is inclosed on the one side by the ridge of the Marboré and the Cylindre, and on the other by the most extraordinary looking mountains I ever beheld. The violence of the winter tempests, and the sudden transitions from cold to heat, and vice versâ, acting upon their limestone formations, had so decomposed their surface, and prevented the growth of vegetation upon a soil, which, but for such causes, would, from its nature, be most productive, as to give them the appearance of mountains of slate rubbish; here and there a band of solid rock was to be discovered; but, in general, the aspect of the mass was that of crumbling decay. Upon the plain of the Millaris, which, almost throughout its whole extent, presents a surface of bare rock, the same operating causes have acted in a different manner. It is rent and cracked in a thousand places; narrow but deep crevices cross it in all directions, most of them filled with water, whilst others, which were dry, allowed us to scan their depth; and over which we had to step, or leap, according to their breadth.

The simple-minded inhabitants of the Spanish valleys believe in a tradition which tells us, that at one period the sterile plain of the Millaris, and the adjoining mountains, were clothed with the most beautiful pastures; but that God, displeased with the shepherds of the district, commanded them to leave them. The poorest of the shepherds obeyed the order; but the rich, disregarding it, a terrible storm was the consequence, whose waters drowned the disobedient mortals, and washed away their pastures. Upon the eve of St. John, the rebellious shepherds are still to be seen wandering among the wilds of the Millaris, vainly searching for their cottages and green fields.

The extremity of the Millaris is closed in by Mont Perdu, whose summit appearing above the collar of clouds which encircled it, seemed a mass of rock floating in the air. The Arragonese seldom call this great mountain *Mont Perdu*, but include it, the Cylindre, and the highest of the towers of the Marboré, under the denomination of *Las tres Sorellas*, or the three Sisters, which, from the Spanish side of the range, are the most decided in character of all the neighbouring summits; and resemble three enormous buttresses which have been placed to sustain the centre of the mountain wall, whose extremities dip into the Atlantic and the Mediterranean.

The hut where we expected to find the Spanish shepherds, and obtain shelter for the night, is not far from the base of Mont Perdu, and thither we accordingly repaired. Neither shepherds nor flocks were, however, near the hut, although from the appearances around it, it was evident that they had very recently deserted it. In the immediate vicinity of the cabin, where the flocks during the period of their sojourn in this Alpine region are assembled each night for safety, the herbage was exceedingly rank and luxuriant, and among the thick grass I observed quantities of molehills, many of them freshly raised. I did not expect to find this little animal at a height of at least seven thousand five hundred feet; and the situation of the place, rendered it a curious circumstance that such a creature should have found its way there. The mole delights in rich and deep soils; and when we do meet with them upon the mountains, it is generally by the sides of the brooks and streams, where the soil has accumulated, and the vegetation is finest; but the little patch of land upon which I observed them at this cabin, was not only situated at this immense height, but it was entirely isolated from the lower pastures by wastes of bare rock of great extent: so that by what instinct the little animal, supposing that he had (as I imagine he must have done) travelled from the plains beneath, could have been induced to undertake so long a journey over the rocks to reach this little oasis, and before arriving at which he must have fasted for many a day, must be a subject of some conjecture.

We had made up our minds to remain at this cabin during the night, and were engaged in collecting the few pieces of wood, the remnants of the shepherds' store, for the purpose of lighting a fire, when Antoine recognized a figure upon the opposite mountain. Rondo was now certain that the shepherds were still among the lower pastures, and as the little heap of wood which we had gathered, would have lasted but a very short time, we proceeded down the mountain, in the

Antoine

London, John Macrone, 1837.

direction of the great gorge of Ordessa. This was lengthening our journey of the morrow very considerably, but fire and shelter at this height, were well worth a slight additional fatigue.

Descending the mountain for a considerable way, we came in sight of another flock, towards which we bent our steps. We soon came up with them, and informed their shepherd of our intention of intruding upon his hospitality for the night, and he, poor fellow, nothing loath to have his solitude broken in upon, even by strangers, most cordially assented. Night was now fast approaching, and the Spaniard had already begun to collect his flock together.

The celerity with which the shepherds of the Pyreneés draw their scattered flocks around them, is not more astonishing than the process by which they effect it is simple and beautiful. If they are at no great distance from him, he whistles upon them, and they leave off feeding and obey the call; if they are far off, and scattered, he utters a shrill cry, and instantly the flock are seen leaping down the rocks, and scampering towards him. Having waited until they have mustered round him, the shepherd then sets off on his return to his cabin or resting place, his flock following behind like so many well trained hounds. Their fine looking dogs, a couple of which are generally attached to each flock, have nobler duties to perform than that of chasing the flock together, and biting the legs of stragglers; they protect it from the attacks of the wolves and bears, against whose approach they are continually on the watch, and to whom they at once offer battle. So well aware are the sheep of the fatherly care of these dogs, and that they themselves have nothing to fear from them, that they crowd around them, as if they really sought their protection; and dogs and sheep may be seen resting together, or trotting after the shepherd in the most perfect harmony. There is no such sight to be witnessed in these mountains as "sheep driving"; no "knowing little collies" used in collecting the flocks, or keeping them from wandering; the Pyrenean shepherd, his dogs, and his flock, seem to understand each other's duties; mutual security and affection are the bonds which unite them. The same confidence subsists between the Pyrenean shepherd and his flock, as that between the shepherd of

Palestine and his, described in the parable of the good shepherd, of whom it is said, "he goeth before them, and the sheep follow him, for they know his voice."

The cabin to which the shepherd conducted us was far superior in comfort, and more dignified in appearance, than the generality of the hovels among the high pastures, whose roofs of stone or turf but very inadequately protect their inmates against the storms of rain and sleet to which they are frequently exposed. It was a small cave, about ten feet square and six high, situated under a great mass of rock, and so secluded among fragments of the mountains, that it would have been difficult indeed for any one, unacquainted with its localities, to discover it. The entrance, originally the full height and width of the cavity, was partly built up with loose stones, and a little doorway left at one corner. Once inside of this dwelling, the storms were not to be dreaded; not even the cold; its being situated nearer the valleys, enabled its owners to procure fuel without very great toil; and the interior being naturally dry, the influence of a good fire was very soon felt within it.

In front of the cave was a platform of mingled rocks and turf, and there the assembled flocks, selecting the most comfortable spots, established themselves for the night; the dogs took their accustomed stations upon the knolls along side, and we entered our place of rest.

The cave was jointly tenanted by the shepherd who had brought us to it, and another, who very soon made his appearance; and whose flock and dogs joined those of the other, without the slightest appearance of dissatisfaction on the part of the first arrived.

We now made preparations for our supper. A bundle of sticks was placed in an angle of the rock, which served for a fire-place, and a light being soon struck, they blazed brightly, and the smoke at once ascending to the roof, passed out of the cave, giving us as little annoyance as would the most perfect chimney. We shared our provisions with the shepherds, and they in return cooking in their copper pot (the only culinary utensil which they possessed) a larger quantity than usual of their customary fare, a soup made of fat, salt, and very black bread, divided it with us.

Of the many times which I had slept in the huts of the Pyrenean shepherds, I had certainly never been so comfortably lodged as upon this occasion, or had more reason to be satisfied with my situation. With a roof over me, impervious to the storms, a cheerful fire, plenty of provisions, a right good appetite to diminish them, and the prospect of climbing Mont Perdu on the morrow, it was not possible to be discontented. Having finished our supper, and given the remnants to the dogs, who, although they must have scented the eatables, never quitted their posts until called for, I had the copper pot well purified from the greasy influence of its late contents, and converted it to a use to which it had never before been applied. It was now promoted to the dignity of a punch-bowl, and a famous *browst* I made in it, composed of a well proportioned mixture of wine, brandy, sugar, and water. Here there was no cupboard, and of course neither cups nor glasses; and the wooden spoons with which we had ate the soup, could not well supply their place, but the pot was not so very large as to prevent us holding it to our lips, and drinking out of it.

This we did; and I shall never forget the looks of supreme satisfaction portrayed on the countenances of the poor shepherds after they had partaken of its contents. Wine they had seldom tasted, brandy they did not even know by name, sugar they had never seen, and the combination of the whole was to them a nectar of whose delicious qualities they had formed no conception. As the *pot* went round, their dark eyes increased in brilliancy; from being at first shy and silent, they became talkative; so did my guides; and in a jargon, half Spanish, half French, many traditionary stories, incidents, and adventures were related on both sides.

These shepherds were among the number of those who had assisted the sons of the muleteer murdered in the Breche de Roland, to carry home their father's body, and from them I learnt some farther particulars relating to the event. From what they told me regarding the appearance of the body, there could be no doubt but that a desperate struggle had taken place between the victim and his murderers; not only was it covered with stabs, but the arms were marked with many deep cuts, such as could only have been received in endeavouring to ward a blow, or given for the purpose of loosing a grasp. The suspicions of the family fell upon no particular individuals; and even if they had, it would have availed little towards bringing the perpetrators of the crime to justice. Civil discord raged over the land, and caused its laws to be broken and trampled upon with impunity.

One of the shepherds had in his possession a knife, found beside the body, stained with blood, and supposed to be that with which the crime had been committed. It was a coarse clasp knife with a wooden handle, and of the largest description which the Arragonese peasantry always carry about with them, the shaft attached to a button hole of their jackets by a piece of cord or ribbon. I had no difficulty in obtaining the knife in exchange for a few francs.

The only real desideratum in this cabin, was a bundle of heath, or rushes to lie upon; these luxuries were not to be procured on the mountain-side, and the shepherds were contented to sleep upon the floor of their dwelling, without any thing to protect them from its flinty inequalities. Capotes and cloaks were, however, put in requisition to promote my comfort; and stretched upon them in the far corner of the cave, with my feet most comfortably placed towards the fire, I was very soon fast asleep.

CHAPTER XVI.

Ascent of Mont Perdu—Its Difficulties—Herd of Izards—Dangerous Paths—Summit—A Mountain View—Formations of Mont Perdu—Lake of Mont Perdu—Respiration at Great Altitudes—Descent of the Mountain—Change of Weather—Dangerous Passage of the Breche de Roland—Difficulty in crossing its Glacier—Descent to the Oule of the Marboré—Its Cataracts—Disbelief of the Aubergiste of Gèdre—Valley of Gavarnie—Pas de L'Echelle—St. Sauveur.

BEFORE day-break, we had left the cabin, and were on our way towards Mont Perdu; and arrived at the base of the mountain about five o'clock. The weather seemed favourable for our enterprise, and the few streaks of clouds which hung around some of the higher summits, did not appear to the guides portentous of a change.

The most remarkable feature which is first passed in the ascent is the Tour de Gollis, an immense circular and altogether inaccessible rock, many hundred feet in height, resembling— as its name denotes—a huge tower, entirely detached from the masses of the great mountain. The path skirting along the base of this solitary protuberance then enters upon a high sloping terrace, composed of the débris of decayed rocks.

This, the first of the series of terraces, which, rising one above another, form Mont Perdu, is succeeded by a deep ravine which separates it from the great band of solid rock which supports the second terrace; at whose base the difficulties of the ascent may be said to commence. A slight fissure in the rock affords the means of scaling it, and of arriving at a slaty slope of the same character as the preceding. Several lower terraces, and projecting rocks, are then scrambled over; among which we came suddenly upon a troop of izards. After the first surprise, they turned round and gazed at us, evidently more astonished at having the solitude of their fastnesses broken in upon, than afraid of our injuring them. Antoine shouted, and they trotted quietly on before us towards the only pass, which, at the extremity of the acclivity upon which we found them, led to the summits of the heights above. This incident, supposing that we had been quite ignorant of the existence of the single route to the crest of Mont Perdu, would have discovered it to us; and, from the casual circumstance of meeting a few izards, we should at once have been enabled to reach that goal which the illustrious Ramond had so long unsuccessfully endeavoured to reach, and which he, and the father of Rondo, had encountered so many hardships and dangers ere arriving at.

This little pass, and the ridge to which it led, although not generally esteemed the most dangerous part of the ascent, was, nevertheless, at the time we passed it, by far the most insecure. The heights by which the troop of izards had passed over, are separated from the last great summit of Mont Perdu by a narrow ravine; and they, and the extremity of the acclivity, or terrace from which they are ascended, form the wall which, upon the southern side, incloses it.

These heights are only accessible by a natural ladder of projecting pieces of rock, which start from the outer edge of the platform beneath. From this spot,—from the first steps of the ladder,—I could look over a precipice perhaps a thousand feet high, and so very perpendicular that, by way of plumbing it, I made Antoine bring me a large stone, which we rolled over, and then, watching its fall, could distinctly see it arrive at the bottom, without once having touched the rock from which we cast it. Climbing this ladder, we reached its ridge, along which we had to wend our way until we gained its highest point; from which it was possible to descend, by means of a similar ladder, into the upper part of the ravine.

The walking along this ridge was exceedingly inconvenient. Its breadth varied throughout its whole length from five to eight feet; its surface was but indifferently *macadamized* with loose stones; the precipices dropped away on both sides; and the wind, unbroken by any height, or mountain to the south, threatened to transplant us into the ravine. The rough surface would not permit us to crawl along upon our hands and knees, and it was impossible to walk upright, and keep from stumbling among the stones. Rondo-proposed that we should link our arms together, and then, steadying each other, walk along the ridge abreast. I did not accede to this plan; because, if one of us *did* chance to stumble, the others would have been pulled down by the falling man, and the whole have perished; whereas, by going singly, each one depended upon himself, and could not endanger the safety of the others. This decided, we proceeded, bent double, so that we might present as little surface as possible for the wind to strike upon; halting, and resting our hands upon our knees when the fiercer gusts swept over us. We thus *sneaked* along the ridge in safety; and, sheltered from the wind on its northern side, descended into the ravine.

The upper story of Mont Perdu now rose before us, and we soon crossed the head of the ravine, and arrived at its base, and at that part of the ascent esteemed by many who had mounted it, the most dangerous; and before the difficulties of which not a few of the aspirants to reach its summit, had shrunk back dismayed. Circumstances which I shall shortly mention, made it appear to me the easiest part of the whole route. Rondo, by way of preparing me for our last escalade, had not ceased to warn me of its difficulty, and to paint its dangers, with what degree of truth, I shall leave the reader to judge. This highest story of Mont Perdu is, towards the south, a circular and perpendicular mass of rock, the lowest part of which, about a hundred feet in height, is situated at the highest point of the ravine, the ridge of which is a line of precipices uniting the heights from which we had descended with this, the wall of the last terrace; and from the spot where the junction takes place, there is distinguished a slight rent from the top to the bottom of the wall of rock which rises above it. This rent is the path to the summit. The waters of the snows above have, in time, worn this fissure, sometimes unscaleable by reason of the stream which pours down it; sometimes from the coating of ice with which it is covered. To the right of the fissure, and within a foot of its edge, the precipices drop away, and far below is seen a great basin of snow and glaciers extending from it to the summits of the ridge which overlook the lake of Mont Perdu.

There was no great quantity of water tumbling

down the fissure; just sufficient to cool our faces, and put us upon our guard against the slipperiness of the wetted rock. Rondo led the way; and I, waiting until he had reached the top, followed. The fissure is in shape angular, and the inequalities of its surface, which renders it accessible, being situated upon both sides, the person who climbs it, having a foot and a hand upon each, is far more secure from danger than when climbing a much less steep *face* of rock. I, therefore, thought the ascent comparatively easy, and being accustomed to consider myself perfectly safe whenever I could lay my hands on any thing which could sustain my weight, (thanks to my early instruction in gymnastics,) I was very soon along side of Rondo, and at the summit of Mont Perdu.

The crest of the mountain is covered with loose stones of small size, and towards the French side is bordered by a parapet of snow five or six feet in height. My first impulse was to turn round and look down upon the route by means of which we had arrived at this great altitude; but it could only be traced for a short distance, the rest was hidden behind the ridge upon which we had found the wind so unpleasant. The mountains and valleys of Arragon were then glanced at; but the mist circling through them, and the heavy clouds driving over them, permitted me to have but a very imperfect view of the great district of Spain visible in clear weather from Mont Perdu; but it mattered not, I had already beheld it from the Breche de Roland.

There was, however, neither cloud nor haze to lessen the extent or diminish the outline of the magnificent range of the Pyreneés, over which to the north, to the east, and to the west, the eye could wander unobstructed. The snow-capped summits of its mountains, their rugged peaks, as countless in number as fantastic in their forms, chequered the vast expanse around me, whose horizon my powers of sight alone could limit. In this waste of ether in which the "everlasting hills" appeared like so many rocks and islands, I could recognise among the great assemblage, the tops of those which, boasting a gorgeous prospect, yet gave me but a faint idea of the glorious spectacle which I now beheld; others whose rocky summits, although far beneath that upon which I stood, had never been pressed by human foot;

others, among whose steeps and forests I had followed the izard, or sought the bear, and in the valleys at whose base I had joined in the sports and dances of the peasantry; others whose names and whose features were familiar to me; but hundreds whose peaks I had never seen, or having seen, forgotten. Mont Perdu is not a giant surrounded by pigmies: a few feet of superiority of height over many of the neighbouring summits is all that it can boast; but that little is sufficient to entitle it to the honours which it bears, and to be esteemed next to the Maladetta, the noblest mountain of the Pyreneés.

Those who wish to have one of the finest views in Europe, of mingled plain and mountain scenery, of river and of sea, must stand upon the summit of the Canigoû; and if they attain its crest under such favourable auspices as I did, I promise that the most greedy *view-hunters* of them all will leave it satisfied with the beauty and magnificence of the prospect. Those, again, who delight to view nature in her more lonely solitudes, and to find themselves in those regions so far above the world, that the pleasures which they enjoy are no longer those of earth; where loftier thoughts and imaginations take their place, where their own insignificance as human beings appears in strong reality, and where feelings of omnipotence and eternity dislodge all others, may be gratified upon the pinnacle of Mont Perdu.

To another class of individuals, to those who would fain fathom the mysteries of the world's formation, and reconcile the various irreconcileable hypotheses which have been propagated regarding it; who would attribute the existence of its mountains to the operation of internal fires, to the depositions of the waters, or other causes, Mont Perdu cannot fail of being an object of great interest. The circumstance of its existence sadly puzzled the geologists, who, having agreed that the primitive mountains were those composed of granite, believed also that the highest summits of the great chains of the European continent, and, among the others, those of the Pyreneés, were formed of the same substance. The observations of the patient and indefatigable Saussure upon the structure of the Alps, had greatly strengthened this idea; the attention of the savans was drawn to the appearances of those mountains, so simple and so perfect in their formations, while the Pyrenees, where all the known strata existed, where mountains of various matters and substances were resting upon or supporting each other, were deemed unworthy of notice. Ramond, however, turned the tide of observation towards his native mountains, and, by his perseverance, established the fact that Mont Perdu,—notwithstanding its great height,—was a mountain of secondary or tertiary formation, superincumbent upon primitive rock, and superior in altitude to the granitic mountains which rise around it.

From the top of the parapet, or bank of snow upon the northern edge of the summit, is seen the lake of Mont Perdu far beneath, encircled with the immense glaciers which hang upon the sides of the surrounding mountains. From beneath a little mound of stones, Rondo drew forth a small bottle, containing the names of the individuals who had reached the summit of Mont Perdu, since Ramond, in 1802, discovered the path which led to it. The bottle (as was the custom) was then broken, the names of the individuals read over, and that of the author added to the list. The whole were replaced in a fresh bottle, and carefully deposited beneath a rude arch, which we constructed to protect it from the winter tempests; there to remain until the lonely solitude of its resting-place should be again disturbed, and the same ceremony gone through. The difficulty in respiration so commonly supposed to take place at great altitudes, was not here in the least perceptible to me; and, at this elevation of nearly 11,000 feet, I was not sensible of any kind of bodily inconvenience whatever.

The broken clouds which came sweeping over our heads from the Spanish mountains, the avant couriers of the heavy mists which now enshrouded them, warning us that it would be wise to quit our lofty station before it became too dark to see our way down from it, we drank in solemn silence to the memory of the illustrious Ramond, and departed.

The difficult parts of the descent were, in succession, passed in safety, and in less than one half the time which we had taken to make the ascent, we arrived at the base of the mountain. Here we had appointed the Spanish shepherds to meet us, with our provisions and cloaks, which we had left at their cabin; which they did, and we sat down to eat our breakfasts. Before we had done, slight drops of rain began to fall; and, looking up towards the summit we had so lately stood upon, it was too evident that we had not left it a moment sooner than we ought to have done, for it was already obscured from our sight among dark and rainy clouds, which, curling along the ridge of the Marboré towards the Breche de Roland, threatened to prevent our passing through it, and to fulfil the prediction of the Aubergiste at Gèdre, that we should find it impossible to return until the next day. But we could not well remain another night with the Spaniards, even should it be considered prudent to do so; our stock of provisions was consumed, and that of the poor shepherds was too small to permit of their sharing it with us, though willingly inclined.

We accordingly parted from them, and set off on our way to the Breche. The rain, descending in torrents, soon drenched our clothes; and, to add to the discomfort which it occasioned, our wine-skin and brandy-flask were both empty. "N'importe!" we could do without them; our blood was neither so old or stagnant in our veins that exercise could not circulate it; and, of this sovereign antidote to cold, we should have ourselves to blame if we had not enough.

The plain of the Millaris, and the crumbling sides of the Marboré,—now more slippery and dangerous than before,— were crossed, and we entered the deep gorge below the Breche. Rondo shook his head at the unpropitious-looking aspect of the pass. The gorge was nearly filled with mist; and of the Breche we could see nothing. Its walls and towers were shrouded in deepest gloom; but the wind, driving the mists furiously along the lower summits, in the direction of the great aperture above, gave us a faint conception of the hurricane we should find in it. Rondo asked me, if I would attempt the passage; and I answered, that if he did not shrink from making it himself, the sooner we proceeded the better; there was no time for deliberation, for it was very cold.

The haze increased in thickness, and the wind in force, as we ascended the side of the gorge; and, by the time we arrived at the chamber of the murdered Spaniard, the blast was fearful; the loosened stones were rolling down the precipices, and the wall above seemed shaking with its violence. We entered the cave, for a moment, to avoid the storm, while we considered of the best mode of passing through the Breche. This place I had quitted the preceding day, and exposed myself to the scorching sun, rather than look upon its blood-stained walls: four and twenty hours after, wet and cold, I sought its shelter, and felt grateful for its existence.

There was now no time to think about the danger of the undertaking, or the chance of one or all of us, being blown down the glacier, or over the precipice; it was too late to retreat, and advance we must, or remain where we were, and die of cold. Frenchmen, talkative as they are, can be silent on some occasions; and upon this, our arrangements were made as quietly and silently as if we were about to commit an act in which we were afraid of being discovered.

Rondo's plan of walking arm in arm was now adopted, and we sallied towards the Breche. The plan was excellent; no single man could have stood the fury of the blast; and, linked together, we staggered like drunken men before it. The wall of the Breche once gained, we crept through the gateway, clinging to the projections of the rock; until, turning round its flank, we were in a moment completely sheltered from the wind. I had heard the wrathful wind whistling through the rigging of a vessel, and rushing through a forest; but, through this funnel of the mountains, it roared; and, wreaking its fury upon the narrow plain of snow between us and the commencement of the glacier, it carried whole layers of it before it, tossing and whirling them about ere they disappeared in the mist.

Rondo was of opinion that we should find the coating of snow which had so greatly aided us in crossing the glacier the preceding day, washed away by the heavy rains; and he, therefore, proposed that before leaving our present situation, we should fasten on the iron cramps, and be prepared for such an event. This we did, and, linked together as before, we entered upon the snow-bank. Walking abreast in this manner, and bending towards the blast, we gained the lee of the other side of the Breche, as much covered with snow, in our short journey, as if it had been shovelled upon us. We now approached the edge of the glacier, where Rondo's prediction was too truly verified. Its covering of snow was entirely gone, and its bare glassy surface revealed, down which the falling rains and the melting snow formed little streams, adding greatly to the difficulties of the passage.

Among the articles which the preceding day I had stigmatized as useless incumbrances, and treated with contempt, was a small hatchet; yet had we not possessed this little implement, we could not have attempted to cross the glacier. Rondo took the lead, never venturing to put one foot before another until he had first carved a substantial resting-place for it in the steep surface of the glassy track upon which we hung, aware that one false step, or the yielding of a piece of ice would send us, like a shot, down the glacier and over the precipice below it. Slowly and cautiously, therefore, did we wend our way across it, halting every now and then to permit of our leader resting his arm from the fatigues of which we could not relieve him; for having once stepped upon the glacier, it was impossible, without the greatest risk, to pass each other, and consequently Rondo, being in advance, had the whole toil of the scooping out of the footsteps to undergo. Once I tried to relieve him, but in endeavouring to pass he had so nearly slipped away, that the attempt was given up; and thus actually crawling along where the day before I should have thought nothing of running, we reached the extremity of the glacier in safety, and glad I was that we did so, for Rondo was so worn out with the exertion, that I am persuaded had the glacier been fifty or a hundred feet broader, he could not have accomplished the distance.

Here we remained a little while to allow Rondo to rest himself, and then resuming our march, descended into the pastures of Les Serrades. There the mist was less thick, and before we reached the narrow pathway which leads from them into the Oule below, we had passed through the region in which it rested, and could see around us. A momentary glance (for we were far too cold to stand still, and our last halt at the edge of the glacier had severely chilled us) showed me the amphitheatre of the Marboré, its terraces and towers obscured by the dark mist which formed a band all round the circle, and from which, as if it had been a terrible waterspout bursting from the overcharged clouds, the cataract, swoln to triple its former size by the unceasing rains, plunged among the rocks of the basin.

The most slippery and insecure portions of the narrow ledge upon which we were descending were crawled over upon our hands and knees; the descent was completed, and we stood once more within the mighty walls of the Marboré. It was now impossible to cross the streams which flow through the Oule, at the places where we had stepped over them the preceding day, it was necessary to make the tour of the basin, and pass between the great cataract and the precipice from which it rolled. This we did; the waters of the minor falls were then waded through in succession, and we gained the road to Gavarnie.

Rondo was now very much fatigued, and could come on but slowly; I therefore left him and Antoine to follow at their leisure, and set off for Gèdre, where I expected to find my valise, and obtain dry clothes. The astonishment of the innkeeper was great, indeed, when I walked into his kitchen. He would not believe that I had been that morning at the summit of Mont Perdu.

"Bah! bah!" said he, "I suppose you mounted to the Breche de Roland yesterday, slept at Gavarnie last night, and have now walked from there; no one could have dared to cross from the Spanish side to-day."

"Well, well," answered I, "Rondo and Antoine can satisfy you on that point when they arrive, meanwhile, I shall lose no time in changing my dripping apparel." I was disappointed in this object; my valise, it seemed, had been left at Gavarnie, and not at Gèdre, so that I had passed it, and must take the chance of the guides bringing it along with them. The landlord, however, lending me a shirt, I proceeded to bed, there to await its arrival, and indulge in the luxuries of an excellent dinner, which the worthy host, conscious how much I stood in need of its comforts, lost no time in preparing. Two hours afterwards Rondo and Antoine arrived, bearing my valise. I was now released from my prison; and towards evening, the rain having ceased, and the clouds cleared away, I bid my guides (who were "fighting their battles o'er again" by the kitchen fire) good b'ye, and left Gèdre for Luz.

The narrow defile which separates Gèdre from

the sweet little valley of Pragnères, and its pretty meads; the dusky gorge beyond, savage-looking even while the sunbeams play upon it; the famous Pas de l'Echelle, and St. Sauveur, from whose windows hundreds of lights were gleaming, and the music of whose gay dancers came sweeping across the valley, were each in succession passed, and I presently entered the cleanly inn at Luz, where I found my friend; and received the caresses of my fine dog, whom I had been forced to lock up at Gavarnie the preceding morning, to prevent him following me to Mont Perdu.

CHAPTER XVII.

Basin of Luz—Its great Beauty and Fertility—Pic de Bergoms—Church of Luz—Baths of St. Sauveur—Castle of St. Marie—Visit of Burke to the Pyreneés—Valley of the Bastan—Village of Barèges, and its Mineral Springs—Appearances of Barèges in Winter—Curious Method of warming themselves adopted by the Peasantry—Environs of Barèges—Pic de Midi de Bigorre—Lac d'Oncet—Valleys of Estaubé and Heas—Superstition of the Mountaineers—Thunder-storm upon the Tourmalet—Gorge of Pierfitte—Its unequalled Grandeur—Valley of Argeles—Beauty of its Features, and mildness of its Climate—Route to Cauteretz—Cauteretz and its Baths—Hunting Quarters—Port d'Espagne—Lac de Gaube—Melancholy fate of an English Lady and Gentleman—Sorrow of the Peasantry at the Event—Boiling Springs.

THE basin in which Luz is situated, is, with the exception of that of Andorre, perhaps the most beautiful, as well as the most extensive, in the Pyreneés. Encircled by lofty mountains, its sole entrances are through the most profound gorges, and along roads scooped out of their rocky sides, hundreds of feet above the torrents which boil beneath; and where the traveller, shuddering at the dangerous path, or delighting in the wild grandeur of the scenery in which he is, as it were, engulfed, is astonished to find the whole character of the scene suddenly change, and a single turn in the path usher him among the softest and loveliest features of fertility. The mountains, above whose precipices he was suspended, and whose rugged cliffs hung over his head, have now receded, and form the picturesque back-ground to the exquisite little landscape before him.

The circular hollow is variegated with corn-fields, meadows, and every species of tree. Its lower eminences are crowned with clumps of wood, or the ruins of old castles; and the waters of the united Gaves from Gavarnie and Barèges, assuming for a time a character in accordance with the peaceful scenes through which they flow, wind along as if they were unwilling to leave it. Villages and hamlets not only skirt the base of the high mountains which inclose it, but appear spotting their sides, and scattered, half-hidden in the forests, far up among their steeps ; where the industry of the peasantry, applied in a thousand different places, has fertilized the slopes and shelves, mingling the yellow of the ripened corn with the sombre foliage of the pine in those regions which, elsewhere, would be devoted to the heath or the box-plant; and high pastures, or dark forests, struggle among the grey rocks and rugged peaks which overtop the whole.

The village of Luz lies at the foot of the high mountain of Bergons, which forms the southern side of the basin ; and whose summit, upwards of four thousand feet above the plain, commands a most extensive prospect, not only of the surrounding mountains, but of the whole valley of the Lavedan, and the low country beyond it. The access to the top of the Bergons, notwithstanding its height, is so very easy, that, in fine weather, whole cavalcades of gay parties from the adjoining watering-places, may be seen, mounted upon the sure-footed little ponies of the district, winding, without difficulty or danger, up the path which conducts to its summit, there to form some idea of the majesty and grandeur of the great mountains beyond it.

The church at Luz is a curious old massy structure, said to have been built by the Templars. It seems to have been intended to supply the joint purposes of a citadel and a place of worship. The church itself, not only being capable of defence, but surrounded by a high wall, full of embrasures, is sufficiently strong to repel the attacks of predatory bands; and, in troubled times, constitute a place of security in which to deposit the property of the inhabitants. On one side of the building is pointed out the door, in barbarous times the only entrance through which the Cagots* were permitted to come into the church. It is now built up; the cruelty, contempt, and aversion with which these outcasts from society were treated by their fellow-creatures, appear only in the pages of history; and, in like manner, we are led to hope that the prejudice which still exists against them, may in time be softened and eradicated.

* The Cagots are a miserable and proscribed race which exist in the Pyreneés, whose origin has been a subject of much controversy. They are idiots, and have, in general, hideous *goitres*.

There are no baths at Luz; but, as at St. Sauveur, where the mineral springs are situated, the accommodation for strangers is seldom equal to the demand—many persons are obliged to submit to the inconvenience of residing half a mile distant from them; while others, who dislike being jostled on all sides by invalids and cripples, prefer the less beautiful, but more retired situation of the former. Luz has also another recommendation; which is, that houses can be had in it at one half of the exorbitant charges which are made for them at St. Sauveur.

The ruins of the castle of Sainte Marie, which crown a high monticule to the east of the village, are exceedingly picturesque. Their origin is the subject of much controversy among the inhabitants of the district. One tradition ascribes their erection to the Knights Templars; who certainly did, at one time, hold considerable possessions in the Lavedan; and to whom I am inclined to accord the honour of having built, not only the church of Luz, and others which are imputed to them, but the greater part of those situated in the mountains of Bigorre and Bearn. The churches which we *know* to have been built by the Templars, have all the same peculiar form of circular chancel; and, as this characteristic feature marks the holy edifices to which I allude, and it is certain that the Templars did, for a long period, rule among the Pyrenean valleys in which these ancient churches exist, there can be little doubt but that they were erected by them.

Another tradition tells us, that the castle of Sainte Marie was built by the English, in the days of the Black Prince; and that it was one of their last possessions in Bigorre. Of the two traditions, the last is the most probable. First, because the Knights Templars (in this part of the country) did not build castles, but fortified the churches, or the preceptories attached to them. And, secondly, as the sovereignty of this valley,—productive in grain of all kinds,—must have been a matter of infinite importance to the party who so long and so gallantly preserved the castle of Lourdes—which guards the entrance to it—to the English monarchy, after the whole of the county of Bigorre had been reduced, it is natural to suppose that they would have endeavoured, by every means in their power, to retain possession of a place from whose environs they could alone draw supplies.

On this subject, however, we shall be more diffuse when we arrive at Lourdes. Meantime, I shall mention a circumstance which will render the precincts of the crumbling walls of Sainte Marie as dear to many an Englishman as the knowledge that their ancestors once gallantly defended them. They are hallowed by recollections of the great writer on the " Sublime and Beautiful:" of that man of whom Fox could well avow, that he had learnt more from than from all other men and authors; and whose dereliction of early principles, however much we may regret, cannot weaken our admiration for his commanding genius, nor the pride which we feel in calling him countryman. At what particular period Burke visited this part of the Pyreneés I could not discover; certainly, prior to the Revolution, and before the first devastating out-break of its pent-up torrents had so wrought upon his fears, and biassed his judgment, as to have led him to prefer (to use his own words) " the furniture of ancient tyranny, even in rags," than witness the *rush* of the waters of liberty which swept them rudely from their resting-place.

The valley of Barèges,—or, as it is more generally called,—of the Bastan, opens into the basin of Luz beneath the castle of Sainte Marie. It extends towards the Pic du Midi of Bigorre; and is, throughout its whole extent, entirely pastoral, and destitute of cultivation; but beautiful in the vicinity of Luz, with verdant sloping meadows, a profusion of fine trees, and innumerable little corn-mills, their wheels driven by the many rivulets which course down the sides of the mountains which border it, and appertaining to each owner of as much land in the neighbouring communes as would raise a few bushels of grain, and who esteems it necessary to have his own particular moulin, in which he grinds the produce of his garden-field.

The village of Barèges, so celebrated over Europe for the character of its mineral springs, is nearly at the head of the valley; which is so very narrow and confined, as to leave at the spot where it is built, scarce room for a single street of houses and the river. This proximity to the Gave, the most turbulent and impetuous in these mountains, is the source of constant alarm and disquiet to the proprietors of the houses, especially to those who have the misfortune to have their property upon the river side of the village, a considerable portion of which is annually swept away by the torrents. Bulwarks of all kinds have been erected to turn aside the wrathful stream; but so ineffectually, that many people actually build houses for the *season*, and take them down after it is over. This is, no doubt, an expensive proceeding; but the concourse of strangers who flock to Barèges for the benefit of the springs or baths, where the accommodations are so inadequate to the demand, so enormously enhances the value of every thing as to render this temporary house-building a profitable speculation.

Louis the Fifteenth erected a military hospital at Barèges, in which great numbers of wounded officers and soldiers have been healed. The waters are efficacious in various disorders; but are particularly famous for healing wounds. They are clear, but emit an unpleasant smell, and should be drunk upon the spot, otherwise their beneficial properties are greatly injured. The

Peasants of Barèges.

London John Macrone 1837

sudatories, especially that allotted to the poor, a kind of subterranean pond, are most unsightly places.

When I visited Barèges in the winter, the Gave had, as usual, carried away the road, which is in summer an excellent carriage one; the mountains were covered with snow, which lay so many feet deep in the street as to be level with the second stories of the buildings; and I found the population of the place—about thirty individuals in all—assembled for warmth in the subterranean pond alluded to. They were not actually in the water; but they sat in a circle round the great bath; the hot vapours from which, effectually heating the place, enabled the inhabitants to exist in the midst of the cold and desolation which surrounded them. Both men and women were busily engaged in knitting the various scarfs and shawls, the beauty of which is so remarkable; and for which they find a ready sale during the season of the waters.

The season at Barèges is all bustle and confusion. The hills echo to the cracking of the postboy's whip, and the jingling of his horses' bells; the road, the knolls, and mountain-paths, are crowded with gaily-dressed strangers, or the natives in their picturesque costumes, who flock in numbers from Tarbes, Lourdes, Argélèz, and Luz, to supply the wants of the visitors; and mineralogists, geologists, and botanists, are seen swarming like bees among the rocks, and on the mountain-sides.

This portion of the Pyreneés abounds in beauties. At the head of the valley of the Bastan is the magnificent mountain, the Pic du Midi de Bigorre; the Pic du Midi, par excellence, for there are many of the high summits of these mountains which bear the same denomination. Like the Canigoû, it abuts into the plain, and commands a most extensive view, embracing many mountains and valleys, and the whole of the low countries between Tarbes and Mielan. On the road to its summit, which is but a little more difficult to arrive at than that of the Pic de Bergons, is the Lake d'Oncet; one of those still dark tarns so common in the Pyreneés.

Upon the opposite side of the Bastan, and in the direction of Mont Perdu, are many scenes well worth visiting; among them, are the Val d'Estaubé, and its circle, or Oule, more developed but less remarkable than that of Gavarnie. The Val d'Heas, and its Oule and chapel, to which the pilgrimages of the superstitious peasantry are so frequent, and among whose wild scenery the processions of the devotees are so exceedingly picturesque.

In the vicinity of this chapel is the famous Caillou de l'Araye, an isolated block of stone, conspicuous from its immense size and situation: Placed upon the summit of a great mass of débris, it attracts the attention of the stranger, as it has done the homage of the mountaineers. It is the Mount Sinai of their imaginations; they believe that the Holy Virgin appeared to their ancestors in this place, and from the summit of this rock presided at the erection of her chapel in the neighbourhood.

There is a bridle-road from Barèges, which passes over the Tourmalet,—the round-backed mountain which runs across the head of the valley Bastan,—to Bagnères de Bigorre, descending into the valley Campan, by the village of Grip. There are no very striking features along the path; and, excepting as a most convenient means of transit between those two places, it has no claims upon the notice of the traveller, unless he may have crossed it in such weather as upon one occasion I did; and then he will have good reason to remember it. I left Bagnères in the morning, and arrived at Grip, drenched with the heavy rain which was falling. Here the guide whom I had brought along with me from Bagnères, shrunk from the weather, and the stormy appearnce of the Tourmalet, and refused to proceed. In the cabin at Grip, however, I found the mountaineer who is in the custom of conveying the letters from Barèges to Bagnères, who was also on his way to the former village; but, like my own guide, was indifferently inclined to face the storm, and intended to remain until the next day at Grip. I bribed him to come along with me; and, leaving my Bagnerès guide behind, we ascended the Tourmalet.

Only those who have been out in a thunderstorm among the mountains, can form any conception of its terrible character. A thunderstorm in the plains, and a thunder-storm on the mountains, are two very different sorts of phenomena; the former is grand and sublime, absorbing our attention, and fixing our regards; but

Peasant Woman
Lighting the Tourmalet.

London, John Macrone, 1837.

the latter is terrific and appalling. The exploding thunders, reverberating among the defiles and gorges, nigh stun us with their crashings; and the forked lightning, playing among the rocks and all around, forcibly remind us of the uncertain tenure of our lives. With the elements in such fearful mood, and a driving blast of sleet in our faces, we crossed the Tourmalet, more than once congratulating each other, when a sudden gust of wind drove us from the path, that the track over this mountain was not remarkable for those passages where "the father never waits for his son, nor the son for his father."

Proceeding down the Lavedan, we enter the gorge which separates the exquisite basin of Luz from the valley of Argélèz. There is not a more magnificent defile in the Pyreneés than this; certainly not one through which the most timid may wend his way in more perfect security; and free from all sensation of danger contemplate the grandeur and majesty of the pass. It is one of those places which never palls upon the sight; visit it as often as we may, there is always something new to be seen; some feature we had not discovered; or those with which we were familiar wearing a different aspect, are still as novel and interesting as at first. The sides of the defile are precipitous mountains; rising at first perpendicularly from the bed of the river, but afterwards, having just sufficient slope to permit the box and heath, and various other shrubs and bushes, and a profusion of wild flowers to hang upon their steeps, even where there appears not a particle of soil to yield them nourishment. The numerous twists and bendings of the defile are still more interesting. There little ravines appear, down which the waters from the upper valleys are seen descending, half hidden in the foliage of the ash and oak trees which skirt their torrents and bend over them; while far above are caught glimpses of the higher regions of the mountains, covered with pines.

The road, by means of which alone the traveller, nay, even the peasant of the district, has been enabled to enter this extraordinary scene, has been a work of prodigious labour. For almost the whole length of the pass, it has been formed by blasting the precipice into galleries, two, three, and sometimes four hundred feet above the river; sometimes forced by an elbow of the mountain to cross to the opposite precipice, there to be forced back again by a still greater obstruction. These crossings and recrossings of the stream, add greatly to the picturesque beauty of the defile; one moment we are in a spot to which the sun's rays scarcely ever find their way, in the next, we have them beating down upon us in all their splendour; and from the centre of the many marble bridges of one arch, which span the dark abyss, the full grandeur of the scene is developed. Such is the gorge of Pierrefitte; fifty years ago an izard could not have clung to its sides, now carriages of all descriptions pass along the fine road which has been constructed through it.

The valley of Argélèz, to which the gorge of Pierrefitte is the magnificent approach upon the south, is, like the basin of Luz, a combination of the beautiful, the picturesque, and the sublime; its plain, far greater in extent and width, presents the same richness of cultivation, diversified with wood and water, as the former; and the mountains which inclose it the same appearance of industry, transforming the wilds into gardens and corn fields. Ancient monasteries, ruined castles, and solitary chapels are distinguished among the woods, beautifying the landscape, and adding greatly to its interest. The woody dells, and deep recesses of many lateral valleys may be scanned from different parts of this Eden of Argélèz; and the dark entrances of the gorges of Cauteretz and Pierrefitte, the town of Argélèz, and its massy church, and the varied forms of the mountains which inclose it, are but a few of its most prominent features. Situated a thousand feet below the basin of Luz, and sheltered by the surrounding mountains, the climate of this valley is exceedingly mild; milder even than in lower situations beyond the outer range of the Pyreneés. When I passed through it in winter, a short time after the severest storms, and when the gorge of Pierrefitte, the basin of Luz, and the surrounding country were buried in snow, the plain of Argélèz and its lower slopes were totally free from it, and green and beautiful as if it had been spring. With such a temperature, the valley of Argélèz is a perfect orchard, abounding in fruits of every description.

The village of Pierrefitte is situated at the entrance of the gorge of Cauteretz, where the road leading to the gay little watering-place of the same name leaves the valley of Argélèz. The scenery along this route is somewhat similar to that of the gorge of Pierrefitte, although not to be compared to it in magnificence. The gorge of Cauteretz is more open; the road does not always hang over its torrents; and the gentler beauties, the little grassy platforms which now and then appear in it, studded with magnificent trees, may render it more pleasing to many individuals than the savage grandeur of the gorge of Pierrefitte.

Cauteretz is built in the hollow formed by the junction of the valleys of Lutour, Cauteretz, and Camp Basque, and in the vicinity of some of the finest scenery and highest mountains of the Pyreneés. Next to Bagnères de Bigorre, it is the most fashionable watering-place of these mountains, and preferable as a place of residence to most of them; at least of those which adjoin the valley of the Lavedan. It is sometimes so very full of visitors, that it is impossible to find accommodation; and, unlike most of the Pyrenean watering-places, it is not deserted during winter, but inhabited by a population of several hundred inhabitants. There are some of the best chasseurs of the mountains natives of Cauteretz, and it is one of the places in which I would recommend those who are fond of such wild sports as izard and bear shooting, to establish themselves for a fortnight, towards the end of spring; and where I can assure them that they will have themselves to blame if they do not meet with success. There is no scarcity of izards upon the neighbouring mountains, and the bears, not now so plentiful as they were, are still to be found among the pine forests which lie between the Vignemale and the Pic du Midi d'Ossau*.

The baths of Cauteretz are situated at a considerable distance from the town, higher up the valley, and upon the sides of the mountain, where their Grecian porticoes, their esplanades, and terraces, appear somewhat out of place among the pine forrests and rugged steeps. The invalids, who cannot perform the distance from the town

* Jean Listapis is the most successful chasseur, and the best guide in this district. Few seasons have passed over in which Jean has not been able to increase the number of notches upon the stick which records his victories over the bears. Implicit confidence may be placed in his honesty, sagacity, and hardihood.

to the baths on foot, are carried in *chaises à porteurs;* fifty or sixty of which strange looking palanquins may be seen plying during the forenoon, along the path by the river side; while the poorer classes, who cannot afford the luxury of such conveyances, are trundled along in wheelbarrows or puny diligences. Some Parisiens of distinction having selected Cauteretz as their place of sojourn during the summer months, it has acquired a character for *good society;* and has consequently become a refuge for the fashionable ennuyé, as well as for the delicate in health, and the infirm. These, to the *healthy* visitor, or traveller, are the disagrémens of most wateringplaces; but at Cauteretz, and other of the mineral sources of the Pyreneés, the sphere of their annoyance being generally limited to the narrow streets of the town, or the gravelled walks and shady places of its environs, they are easily avoided, and their existence forgotten in the solitude of the neighbouring mountains.

Beyond the baths, but in the same valley, that of the Marcadaon, is the cascade of the Pont d'Espagne, the beau ideal, in the mind of the water-drinkers and fashionables of Cauteretz, of a mountain waterfall; and at the head of the valley, to the left of the Pont d'Espagne, is the Lac de Gaube. It was in this lonely lake, embosomed among the solitudes of the great Vignemale, whose hanging glaciers and lofty cones rise in all their majesty upon its southern side, that an English lady and gentleman, who had been but a few weeks married, were drowned. There is a little skiff upon the lake, belonging to the fisherman who occupies the hut on its bank, and gains a livelihood by catching the trout in which it abounds, and selling them to the hotel-keepers at Cauteretz. The unfortunate couple determined to sail round the lake in this skiff, which could only carry two. The lady stepped in first, and the gentleman, pushing the boat from the shore, made a spring to follow her. He was unsuccessful, the skiff had shot away too far, and he plunged into the water. The lady, in endeavouring to seize her sinking husband, lost her balance, and was precipitated into the lake, in whose deep dark waters they both instantly sank. The melancholy fate of these individuals was at the period of the event a source of much weeping and wailing among the peasantry of the district, and even now they never talk of it without expressing their sorrow at the untimely death of the young strangers.

Besides the springs which supply the baths, there are various others, which issue, scalding hot, from the rocks by the side of the Gave; and in winter, when the whole scene was one dreary waste of snow, it was a strange and curious sight to observe the waters boiling from their sources, and steaming as they united with the nigh freezing waters of the stream.

Retracing our steps down the gorge of Cauteretz, and through the charming valley of Argélèz, beautiful at all times and in all seasons, we enter the defile which separates it from Lourdes.

CHAPTER XVIII.

Defile of Lourdes—Castle of Lourdes—Its History interesting to Englishmen—Its gallant Defence by Ernault de Bearn—The Chivalry of France driven from before its Walls—Assassination of Ernault—Continued Defence of Lourdes by his Brother—Route from Lourdes to Pau—France Pittoresque—St. Pe—Betharam—Pilgrimages to its Calvary—The mingled Devotion and Hilarity of the Peasantry—Plain of Bearn—Chateau of Corraze—Veneration of the Bearnais Peasantry for the Memory of Henri Quatre—Pau—Its Attractions—Splendid View of the Mountains—Society of Pau—Hanoverian Baron—Anecdote of George the Third and Queen Charlotte—Anecdote of a German Soldier—Origin of Pau—Bernadotte, King of Sweden—Climate of Pau.

THE defile of Lourdes,—the approach, on the one side to the wild and interesting beauties of the Pyreneés, on the other to the rich and sunny plains of Bearn,—acquires, from its situation, a degree of credit to which its own peculiar features would not entitle it. The mountains which enclose it are tame and destitute of wood; the débris of their immense slate-quarries blacken the pastures; and the Gave, which winds beneath, no longer pent between opposing cliffs, luxuriates in indolence. The scenery improves after we have mounted the steep ridge in the vicinity of Lourdes, and can look down upon the environs of its ancient castle, the *Mirambel* of the Saracens, and the stronghold of the adherents of the Black Prince in his county of Bigorre.

Although the inhabitants of this district are not unfrequently denominated "les petits fils des Anglais" by the neighbouring peasantry; and although it was the scene of many of the brightest deeds of ancient chivalry connected with the English name; still, every French author who has written upon this part of the Pyreneés, has, either wittingly or unwittingly, abstained from even alluding to that period when it formed a part of the appanage of the princes of Wales, or noticing the persevering gallantry displayed in retaining it under their sovereignty. From this silence on the part of the only writers who give any account of the district, few of my countrymen unacquainted with the history of the times of the Black Prince are aware, while they admire the fine situation of the castle of Lourdes, and the gorgeous scenery which surrounds it, that there was a time when the banner of England floated from its towers, when the élite of France could not pluck it from its resting-place; and when its defenders, deserted upon all sides, with not a foot of territory but the barren rock upon which the fortress was built, and without a hope of succour from their distant sovereign, defied their enemies, drove them from their walls; and, for a long series of years, displayed a bravery which no dangers could appal, and a fidelity to their Prince which has no parallel in history. Under such circumstances, a short summary of our dominion in Bigorre may not be deemed uninteresting.

The county of Bigorre, which comprised nearly the whole of the country between the kingdom of Bearn, and the district of Foix, was rendered to Edward III. as the price of the freedom of John, King of France, taken prisoner at the memorable battle of Poictiers. Edward, in 1362, bestowed the Duchy of Aquitaine—of which the county of Bigorre formed a part—upon his son, the Black Prince; who, in the following year, accompanied by his princess, left England, to take possession of his continental dominions.

Bordeaux was the capital of his duchy, and the seat of his government; but the Count of Armagnac, captivating the fancy of the royal pair with the description which he gave to them of the beauty of their distant little kingdom in the Pyreneés, and of its flourishing capital, Tarbes, persuaded them to visit it. Accordingly, they came to Tarbes, where they remained for a considerable time, and held their court, at which the whole of the neighbouring princes assembled to do them honour.

The Black Prince, delighted with his mountain province, made excursions through its various valleys; in some of which he built new fortresses, in others, strengthened those which existed. With the structure of that of Lourdes he was particularly pleased, and at once perceived the great benefit which would accrue to him from a continued possession of it. " It is," said he, " the key of many countries, and from it I can find my way into Arragon, Catalonia, or Barcelona." Its fortifications were immediately improved, and the command of the place given to Pierre Ernault, a native of Bearn, a cousin of the Count of Foix, and an individual upon whose fidelity the Prince thought he could rely. Upon bestowing this government upon Ernault, the Black Prince said to him, " Master Pierre, I constitute and appoint you captain of Lourdes, and warden of Bigorre; see that you preserve them, and render a good account of them to my father and myself." The Prince, having regulated the government of his province, and intrusted its defence to those in whom he thought he could confide, shortly after broke up his court at Tarbes, and returned to Bordeaux.

No events of importance took place in Bigorre, and the Prince's right to its sovereignty remained undisputed, until the war broke out between France and England, in 1369. Several of its barons, bribed with French gold, then deserted to the enemy, and delivered up their castles, which they had sworn to defend: and the approach of the Duke of Anjou, at the head of an army composed of the best soldiers of France, terrified others into submission. The governors of Mauvoisin,

Lourdes, and other places, however, indignantly refused the bribes tendered them, and bade defiance to the French host. Mauvoisin was first attacked, and was (as I have before mentioned) gallantly defended; and honourably surrendered, when the means of defence were at an end. Tarbes was treacherously given up by its governor, and the Duke laid siege to Lourdes.

The castle of Lourdes is built upon an immense rock, which rises from the centre of a hollow, or basin, formed by the surrounding hills. The Gave of Pau, issuing from the gorge leading to Argélèz, flows round its western base, thus adding to the strength of the place; while the other sides of the rock are almost inaccessible; and, in olden times, must have been rendered completely so by the walls and towers which rose from them.

The first efforts of the besiegers were directed against the town, which hangs upon a slope to the east of the castle; and which, for fifteen days, baffled their utmost exertions to take it. At the end of which time, the governor, having withdrawn the whole of the inhabitants, and lodged them within the walls of the castle, the Duke of

Anjou, amid great rejoicings, took possession of the deserted houses. He could, however, make no impression upon the castle. Day after day for six weeks was the assault renewed, but all to no purpose; the garrison remained uninjured; and his own soldiers were driven back with great loss from every attempt, although supported by the showers of stones which were hurled upon the besieged from the "*grands mangonneaux*," constructed by the orders of the Duke.

Despairing of success by open warfare, the Duke redoubled his exertions to seduce Pierre Ernault from his allegiance to England, proffering him vast sums of money, and many estates: but ineffectually; his integrity was incorruptible. "The garrison is not mine," said Pierre to the envoy of the Duke; "and the property of the King of England I cannot sell, alienate, or give away, without proving myself a traitor; which I will not, but remain faithful to my liege lord, upon whose hand, when he appointed me governor of this castle, I swore by my faith to defend it against all men, and to yield it to no one who had not his authority to demand it from me; and Pierre Ernault will keep his oath until he dies.

Carry this answer to your master; no other shall he ever receive from me." At last, the Duke of Anjou, finding that all his attempts to batter down the walls of Lourdes, or corrupt the honesty of Ernault, proved abortive; raised the siege, and retired, mortified and disgusted with his ill success.

But, although Ernault had thus gallantly defended the castle of Lourdes against the French army, and forced it to retire with disgrace from before its walls; he had still another, and more dangerous enemy to dread, whose most anxious wish was to obtain possession of the fortress; and whose proximity to the place gave him every opportunity of pouncing upon it in some unguarded moment. This enemy was his cousin, the Count of Foix and Bearn. Prior to the repulse of the Duke of Anjou, the Count had never openly expressed his wish to become master of Lourdes; but, shortly after that event had taken place, he sent to Ernault, and requested him to come to Orthès, as he wished to have some conversation with him, regarding the state of the country. Ernault, dreading no evil on the part of the Count, although not altogether unconscious of his designs, at once consented to the proposition.

Previous, however, to leaving Lourdes, he assembled the garrison together, and appointed his brother to the command of the castle in his absence. "John," said he to his brother, "the Count of Foix has sent for me, with what intention I do not know; but, if it is true that the Duke of Anjou and he have been entering into an alliance, and he seeks this interview for the purpose of getting me to surrender the castle to him, I shall in such case tell him, as I did the Duke, that while I have life the castle of Lourdes shall never belong to any one but the King of England. And you John, who are now to take my place, swear to me by your faith and noble birth, that you will guard it as I have done, and never yield it to another than he who entrusted it to us."

John swore as desired, and Ernault proceeded to Orthès; where, a few days after his arrival, the Count of Foix made a formal demand of the castle of Lourdes; urging, as a reason for his doing so, that the Duke of Anjou had stated, that he (the Count of Foix) had caused the failure of his expedition against that place by the support which he gave to the besieged; and, although this suspicion of the Duke's was perfectly unfounded, still, as he did not wish to incur the displeasure of so great a prince, he deemed it prudent to acquire possession of Lourdes.

Ernault undauntedly replied, though surrounded by enemies, among whom were many of the rebel barons of Bigorre—" Sir, I owe you duty and regard because I am a poor chevalier of your blood and country; but the castle of Lourdes I cannot yield to you. You have sent for me; I am here; and you can do with me what you please: but that which the King of England has entrusted to my care, to him only will I give it up."

" Ha! false traitor," cried the haughty and passionate Count, drawing his dagger—" Do you dare to speak those words to me? By that head thou hast not said them for nothing!"—and he stabbed Ernault to the heart.

" Monseigneur, vous ne faites pas gentilesse,"— said the faithful servant of England,—"vous m'avez mandé, et si m'occiez."

The death of Ernault did not, however, aid the

Count in his attempts to gain possession of Lourdes. John Ernault proved as brave and incorruptible as his brother; and, after the whole of Bigorre had been reduced, either by the French King, or by the Counts of Foix and Armagnac, the castle of Lourdes remained in possession of the English; and its garrison, unsatisfied with being merely able to defend themselves within its walls, were a continual source of dread and annoyance to their powerful neighbours, into whose territory they continually broke; and, while the armies of England were contending in the northern parts of Aquitaine and France, they carried terror and dismay through the counties of Carcassone, Toulouse, and the Albigeois.

The numerous little forts, the ruins of which appear in all the smaller valleys in the vicinity of Lourdes, were the watch-towers which gave notice to the garrison of the approach of enemies, and secured to them, from the fertility of the districts in which they were situated, an abundant supply of provisions. These dependent fortresses often fell into the hands of the enemy, who wreaked their vengeance on them when they did not dream of attacking the castle of Lourdes,—" Car Lourdes étoit un chastel impossible à prendre." And so it proved during the many changes of fortune which the English dominion in the south of France underwent; for the banner of England spread its folds in the Lavedan long after it had been torn from the strong places of Guienne and Gascony; and was not lowered from the citadel of Lourdes, until the English monarch renounced all right to these provinces.

The route from Lourdes to Pau lies along the banks of the Gave, which, sweeping round the outer ridge of the mountains, winds along their base. Here, although we are no longer among the mountains, we have something more to interest us than the recollections of their delightful valleys; for the aspect of the country, though changed in character, is still beautiful; and, after a long sojourn among scenes more wild and sublime, would charm even by its novelty. The river has now become a noble stream; and the rocky walls which confined its waters have been succeeded by green and wooded hills; farmhouses, orchards, and cottages, surrounded by oaks of "a hundred years," and magnificent walnut trees skirt its banks, and waving cornfields: the appearance of Indian corn,—the most gorgeous of all crops,—the increasing influence of the sun, and the absence of the cool breezes which neutralize his rays, indicate our near approach to the richest plains of the south; and that portion of the French empire to which the epithet "La belle France," can with truth be applied.

France, I believe, has been compared to an ugly picture set in a beautiful frame; and, from my own observation, I should not hesitate to say, that the simile is a most correct one. Some few spots there are, no doubt, in the interior of the country, well worthy of admiration; but, for how many hundred miles must we travel to reach them, and how distant are they from each other! and, after all, when they have been discovered, who that has gazed upon the surpassing beauty and magnificence of the frame, and the varied character of its workmanship, will not agree with me in declaring that those natives and foreigners who have formed their opinions of "France pittoresque" from the scenery on the banks of the Loire, (the "garden of France," as a part of it is absurdly styled,) or any, or all of the "charming spots" so thinly scattered through the interior of that extensive country, can have but a very inadequate conception of the high rank which France, by reason of the glorious frame in which she is encased, is entitled to hold among picturesque countries.

After passing the curious old town of Saint Pe, whose monastery was founded in 1032, by William, Duke of Gascony, the hills upon the right of the road become gradually lower, until, at Betharam, they have entirely disappeared, and the rich plains of Bearn stretch out before us. Betharam is a college for the education of young priests; and famous throughout the surrounding country for the pilgrimages which are made to the Calvary, situated upon the little wooded hill which surrounds it. The sanctity of this spot is very great, and throughout the whole season, numbers of devotees may be seen winding their way up the steep ascent of the mount, kneeling, and repeating the prescribed Pater and Ave, at the various *stations*, or chapels, in which are most extraordinary and grotesque-looking groups of figures in wood, intended to represent the passion of our Saviour.

In the month of September, when the *fête de la Vierge* attracts the whole population of the country to this holy hill, the scene which the place presents is of the most curious description. The roads, and fields, and woods seem then alive with dense masses of human beings, all directing their steps towards the Calvary of Betharam. The various colours of their picturesque costumes, —the gay capulets of the women, the flowing sashes of the men,—and, above all, the chanting of their hymns, which they sing in chorus, render the spectacle animating and interesting. A long line of tables fringes the bottom of the ascent, covered with holy trinkets of every kind,—rosaries, crosses, rings, and amulets, all blessed by some holy father, nay, even by the Pope himself, if we were to believe the assurances of the venders: at which each pilgrim makes a purchase according to his faith or his ability.

The ascent of the Mount is then made; some parties displaying their devotion by performing the journey barefoot, or on their knees; others, whose sins hang less heavily on their consciences, hurrying over the ceremony as fast as possible, that they may return to their friends, who, having already piously relieved themselves of their sins, are rejoicing over the event in the village below. Feasts are prepared in all the cabarets, and there the sad and weary pilgrims of the morning, disburdened of their last year's load of sins, are transformed into light-hearted and joyous peasantry; the sacred hymn into the convivial glee; and every countenance is beaming with gladness.

Towards evening, groups are seen assembled under the trees, dancing to their rustic music, or singing in bands; and, when the day of mingled penance and rejoicing is drawing to a close, the various parties wend their way homewards, still singing and rejoicing, and completely forgetting the vexations or misfortunes of the year gone by, in their anticipations of the happiness of the ensuing one.

From Betharam to Pau, the country is a perfect garden in cultivation; and the inhabitants preferring to associate together, rather than reside in scattered hamlets and cottages, the road is almost a succession of villages and houses. One of the largest of these is Corraze, a few miles from Betharam, upon the heights above which, are the ruins of the chateau in which the younger days of Henry the Fourth were passed, and where by the hardy life which he led, and joining in the games and sports of the peasantry, he inured his body to fatigue, without which he could not have survived the hardships of his riper years, and acquired the love of his subjects, who never failed him in the hour of need, nor deserted him in his misfortunes. "I would," said the young prince of Bearn, ever anxious for the welfare of his people, "that the poorest peasant of my country could put a fowl in his pot upon Sunday." And they had never cause to lament the futility of his promises. His memory is still idolized by the people, and although "les murs qui l'ont abrité, les edifices qu' il a construits, disparaîtront; mais la memoire de ses hautes qualités, de ses bienfaits, ne s'effacera plus. Voilà le sol qu' il a longtemps foulé de ses pieds nus; les montagnes, les bois qu' il a souvent gravis, haletant et couvert de sueur; et les hameaux, ou pressé par la faim, il se réfugiait pour manger la pâte ou la millade du paysan beárnais, qui partageait gaiment avec son

Henri." Few kings were so well beloved by their people as the Prince of Bearn; and still fewer have left behind them so good a name as the "bon Henri."

From Corraze to Pau is but a very short distance; and this, the ancient capital of the Bearn, is beautifully situated upon a high terrace overlooking the Gave, and commanding a fine prospect of the surrounding country. Pau is not only interesting on account of the many historical recollections connected with its name, and the distinguished station which, from the earliest periods of European history, its counts, and princes, and kings, have held among the potentates of the continent, and the early institution of a limited monarchical form of government; but, from its situation in one of the richest and most abundant countries in the world; and in one of the finest climates; its environs comprising all the loveliness of vine-clad hills, and sunny dales, green meadows, and fertile fields, and gardens, and copses, and orchards.

These attractions have, for many years, rendered Pau a favourite place of exile to those English who fly to a genial clime in the pursuit of health, or to economize, where markets are excellent, and provisions cheap; and no other town of the south can be compared to Pau for those advantages, for there is none other that can boast a less changeable climate, and where the varied luxuries of a southern climate can be obtained at less expense. The chief desideratum of Pau, as a place of residence, is the want of comfortable houses, such as are to be met with at Tours, and other towns of France where the English colonize themselves. There are few single houses to be had; and *flats*, if disagreeable at home, are ten times more so abroad. The streets of Pau are, besides, inconveniently narrow, and, for a great part of the year, abominably dirty, sadly deteriorating the purity of the pure mountain air which surrounds the town.

There is, however, one section of the town far superior in comfort and appearance to the rest; and there I would advise any one who may decide upon residing in Pau, to choose his abode. This is the south side of the Rue Royale, which is built upon the edge of the terrace above the Gave. There there is less noise and bustle; and the purest air, and the most splendid view to the south, east, and west, that can be imagined. Below is the extensive and wooded plain of the Gave, broad and open to the east and west, where the windings of the river are traced and lost in the distance, but narrowed and contracted to a mile in breadth opposite to the town by the numerous low hills which, running out laterally from the mountains, and divided into numberless small valleys, ravines, and dells, resemble a succession of mighty buttresses, intended as a support for the great mountains behind them. These hills, chequered with copses, and the vineyards from which the red and white wines of Jurançon are produced, and adorned with country houses,— border the noble plains beneath. Higher and more distant hills succeed them; and, above the whole is seen one long-continued range of summits, of most fantastic forms, from the Pic du Midi de Bigorre,—forming a promontory on the east,—to the inferior mountains which, beyond the valley d'Aspe, gradually decrease in height as they approach the ocean. Among the most distant summits to the east may be distinguished the glaciers of the Neouville and the Vignemale, sparkling in the sun; and at the head of the valley d'Ossau, which opens immediately to the south of Pau, the Pic de Gers, the masses of the Eaux Bonnes, and the gigantic fork of the Pic du Midi d'Ossau, the most picturesque-looking of all the Pyrenean mountains, are conspicuous in the outline of this magnificent and unequalled amphitheatre.

The society of Pau, like that of most other towns which is composed of chance visitors, can scarcely be characterized; the general rule, however, which more or less applies to every small continental town in which a few English families have domiciled themselves, is applicable to Pau. A few families constitute a society so limited and contracted, that it is seldom pleasant or agreeable; and, no matter how worthy and excellent the component parts of it may be individually, still, when taken together, they fail in one material point—unity-; and, instead of that good feeling which we should naturally expect to exist among the natives of one country residing in a foreign land, we invariably find the reverse, and the little "body politic" divided into as many sects and parties as there are in the Christian religion; each party, its occupations and amusements, forming a topic of criticism and discussion to the others.

Among the families residing at Pau during the period of my sojourn in the neighbourhood of the Pyreneés, was that of a Hanoverian Baron. From the society of this esteemed individual I derived much pleasure. The Baron's early life had been spent at the court of George the Third, with whom he was an especial favourite, and many an anecdote has he told me of the "good old King's" eccentricities, and very sensible dread of "Charlotte." Although, perhaps, somewhat out of place in these volumes, I cannot resist the inclination to glean a few characteristic incidents from the Baron's recollections of their Majesties.

George the Third, like Frederick William, of Prussia, had a great admiration of tall and handsome men, and seldom selected an aide-de-camp or attendant who was not in stature fit to be a grenadier. Possessed of these essential qualifications together with the advantages of high birth, the Baron became the "shadow" of His Majesty, and in company with another equally well favoured countryman, attended him in his walks; no light duty, considering how very fond he was of pedestrianism. On such occasions His Majesty, when he met with any one who he did not think had seen the Hanoverians, would immediately introduce them, preluding the introduction with such expressions: " Have you seen these gentlemen before?" " Have you ever seen such men?" &c., &c. To be shown off in this manner was sufficiently annoying to my friend, whose companion, on the other hand, enjoyed the distinction. The powers of memory possessed by the royal family of Great Britain are proverbial; George the Third had never resided in Hanover, yet the knowledge which he had of his subjects there, and of their family history, was wonderful, so much so that there was scarcely a single family of distinction with whose history he was not to the full as well acquainted as the family themselves were. The following anecdote displays the goodness of his heart, and the awe in which he stood of his royal spouse. The baron commanded a regiment of cavalry who wore the enormous jackboots then in use. Somehow or other it entered into His Majesty's fancy to have a pair of these boots, and he accordingly applied to the Baron to have them made by the bootmaker of the regiment; and had his measure taken. The bootmaker, either from having little assistance, or anxious to do justice to His Majesty's boots, did not finish them for some days; but so very eager was the King to have them, that he never failed each morning to visit the maker, and to inquire how they were progressing. When they were at last finished, and he tried them on, they fitted so very well, and pleased him so much, that, turning to the bootmaker, he asked him if he had a family. "Yes, your Majesty," answered the man, "I have a wife and family in Germany."

"Very well," said His Majesty, giving him eight guineas, "send that to your family, it may be of benefit to them."

So delighted was the King with his boots, that it was his first desire to display them before the Queen, and, accompanied by the Baron, he made his appearance before her. Strutting forward, and kicking his legs right and left, he said, "Well, Charlotte, what do you think of my boots, are they not beautifully made?" Her Majesty paid the desired compliment, upon which the King whispered, "I gave *four* guineas for them."

One other of the Baron's anecdotes I cannot help also relating. It regards the honesty and integrity of a Hanoverian soldier. In the campaign of ——— a soldier of the German Legion was brought before a court martial, accused of having drawn his sword upon his officer. The fact was proved, and the articles of war awarding death as the punishment in such cases, the soldier was sentenced to be shot. The Baron, who was a member of the court, happening to be acquainted with the history of the man, stated his knowledge of circumstances greatly to the credit of the offender, and obtained leave to mention them. It seemed, that after a previous campaign, and when the greater part of the German Legion was ordered over to England for the winter, many of the officers of that corps, trusting to the honour of their men, allowed them to return home, taking along with them their horses and accoutrements, upon their simple engagement to join their respective regiments when called upon. One reason for granting this indulgence to the soldiers was the great dislike which the Hanoverians had to English barracks. The troops were unexpectedly called out, and in some, although not in many cases, the confidence of the officers in the men was found to have been misplaced. The regiment to which the man before the court belonged, was directed to assemble at a particular port, for embarkation to England; and soldiers on leave received orders to join. Owing to some mistake, the offender had no order sent him to join, and several days elapsed before he accidentally became aware of the circumstance. He, however, lost no time, but mounting his horse, set off for the place of rendezvous. Upon arriving at it, he found that the regiment was gone. He followed it to the coast, at some distance from which he encountered two soldiers of his own corps returning homewards. He accosted them, and inquired if it were not true that the regiment was at a certain port, and that the transports would soon sail. They answered in the affirmative, adding that the vessels had already sailed, and that they, profiting by the confusion, had taken the opportunity to return home.

"Sapperblew!" said he to them, "do you mean to desert?"

"Certainly, to return home," said they.

"Well," answered the individual before the court, "you may desert, but at all events you shall not steal the horses;" and drawing out his pistols, he threatened to shoot them dead if they did not instantly dismount, and give him up the horses. The deserters, well aware of his character for bravery and determination, obeyed him, and resigned their horses. Taking the extra horses along with him, he proceeded to the coast, where he found that the transports had sailed. What was he to do? Was he to return home? No; he would still endeavour to join his corps. Fortune favoured his resolve, for he heard that there was still another transport lying at some distance along the coast, which was waiting for some of the "gentlemen of the Guards." He set off for it, and having reached it, he reported himself to the captain, at the same time stating the circumstances which had prevented him from sailing along with his own regiment. So delighted was the captain of the transport with the soldier's honesty, that notwithstanding that his ship was only intended to convey infantry, he put himself to considerable inconvenience, and received the man and his horses on board.

In the meantime the regiment to which the prisoner belonged, had arrived in England, and upon its muster-roll being called over, each individual who did not answer to his name was noted down as a deserter. When the prisoner's name was called, and not answered to, a corporal of the regiment stepped forward, and requested that he might not be put down as a deserter. "I am certain that he is no deserter," said he, "and that ere long he will make his appearance." The corporal was asked the reasons for his believing that the missing man would return, which, now that the regiment was in England, was so improbable a circumstance. He said, that he was sure that no order to join had been sent to his friend, but independent of this he had another stronger reason for believing that his comrade would return. It seemed that he (the corporal) had, when the regiment was disbanded, given to the missing man the loan of his watch, who for some reason or other wished to make an appearance at home; "and if it was for no other reason than to return me the watch," said the corporal, "I am positive that he will soon be here." Upon this statement the prisoner before the court was not noted down as a deserter. The ship he was on board arrived in England, and being put on shore, and having discovered where his regiment was quartered, he joined it, with the watch and the three horses, to the astonishment of many, but amply justifying the character which the corporal had given of him.

The members of the court martial were so pleased with this simple statement of facts by the Baron, that they unanimously and strongly recommended the prisoner to mercy. I ought to have mentioned, that the crime which the man had been found guilty of, had been committed when in a state of intoxication, and when, from the effects of a severe wound in the head, he became ungovernable. The Duke of York, a short time previous to the sitting of this court martial, had issued an order, that any recommendation to mercy in such cases should not be attended to. The court nevertheless did recommend the prisoner to mercy, and the Duke sent back the proceedings of the court, at the same time desiring it to sit again, and revise the sentence. The court martial sat again, but the articles of war were so decided that they could not find otherwise than they had originally done. The same sentence of death was awarded, but along with it, and regardless of the Duke's order to the contrary, a recommendation to mercy, if possible, still stronger than the former, was forwarded to the commander in chief. The result was, that the sentence was commuted to transportation to the West Indies. The Baron told me that he had once received intelligence regarding the soldier, since he was sent to India, where, in the course of a short period, he had been promoted to the rank of sergeant-major, "but," added the Baron, "I am afraid that the climate, or the strong drink will have killed as fine and noble a fellow as ever wore a sabre."

The town of Pau originated from the circumstance of a chateau being built by one of the princes of Bearn, in the tenth century, to protect his territory from the incursions of the Moors of Spain. For this purpose, he obtained from the inhabitants of the valley d'Ossau, the land upon which to build his fortress, on condition that their descendants should enjoy the privilege of occupying, during the sittings of the national assemblies, the first place in the great hall of the castle which he intended to erect. This right being yielded, three stakes were driven into the ground, to mark the limits of the grant. Stake in Bernais is called *paou;* and, from these stakes, the castle and town which rose around it, derived their name, now corrupted into Pau.

The situation of the castle is at the extremity of the terrace on which the town is built. The ancient fortress of the Princes of Bearn has been succeeded by the more modern chateau of the Kings of Navarre; an irregular mass, flanked by towers and pavilions of unequal height; by no means remarkable in appearance, but rendered sufficiently interesting by historical recollections, and the grandeur of the prospect from its walls. The most antique-looking part of the building is the square tower of brick, near the principal entrance, said to be the birth-place of Henry IV., whose cradle, made of tortoiseshell, preserved in the chamber where it was first used, is a relic dear to every true Bearnais.

Bernadotte, King of Sweden, was a native of Pau; and began his career of life as apprentice to a baker. In 1780, he became a soldier; and, in 1818, "*il passa roi*"—the expression used by the soldiers of the empire, as accustomed to see their commanders made kings as generals. The house in which he was born is situated in one of the inferior streets of the town, and the event is recorded by an inscription over the door. Although Napoleon said, that "Bernadotte a été le serpent nourri dans notre sein;" with what justice is a matter of opinion: still he has not, like most other men who have risen from a humble to an exalted station, been so intoxicated with his prosperity as to forget his poor relations, most of whom he has provided for, and rendered comfortable in life.

The climate of Pau is perhaps the most genial, and the best suited to invalids, of any other spot in France. There are there no such sudden changes, such transitions from heat to cold, as at Nice or Montpellier, nor piercing cold winters as at Tours; indeed, the almost continual fine weather is only broken for three weeks or a month in the beginning of January by the winter rains, accompanied by slight frost; but the snow is seldom visible a few hours after it falls; and the heats of its southern latitude are tempered by the vicinity of the mountains, in whose cool recesses, those who feel the summer sun too oppressive, can in a very few hours take refuge. The nearest watering-places of the Pyreneés to Pau, are the Eaux Bonnes, and the Eaux Chaudes; and thither we shall, in a subsequent chapter, conduct the reader.

CHAPTER XIX.

Pyrenean Horses—Their character—Conjectures regarding the Race—The Haras—Breeding of Horses in the South—The ignorance of the French upon the Subject—Expense and inefficiency of the Haras—Cheapness of Horses—Great Fairs—Horse-dealers—Mode of Bargaining—Spanish Mule-dealers—Their fine Appearance—Number of Mules exported from France into Spain—Price of Mules—String of Mules—Extreme Honesty of the Spanish Mule Merchants—Horse-races in the South—Their Character—Vanity of the French—Description of a Fox-hunt.

IN mountainous districts, we generally find a race of horses, small but active, and, therefore, better suited for the work they are required to perform. Accordingly, along the whole line of the Pyreneés, and even throughout the vast plains which extend from their base, we find a species of small, wiry, and in general, exceedingly ugly animal to predominate. For what length of time this may have been the character of the horse in the most southern provinces of France, it would be difficult to discover; but if I might be allowed, without any authentic information on the subject, to hazard a conjecture, I should suppose that the same description of horse has existed for a very long period. In a country so hilly and mountainous, and where, until very lately, even in the most populous and richest districts, good roads were altogether unknown, the small and active animal was the one most efficient for carrying to market the produce of the country. Almost all the cross-roads are at this day little better than the channels of the streams and rivulets, where even the ox-cart cannot ply its sluggish course. Every article must, therefore, be transported on horseback; and as the horse is seldom or never made use of for agricultural purposes, it is almost certain that from the period when beasts of burden were first required by the natives of the Pyreneés, that the species of horse at present in use there, would be the kind sought after by them.

To Pau, Tarbes, and to all the other towns in Bearn and Bigorre, three parts or more of the corn, maize, and other produce of the country are brought to market upon the backs of horses, hundreds of which may be seen, upon market-days, passing along the roads, each carrying its complement of sacks. Divided as the soil is into small proprietorships, each owner of an arpent of land possesses a horse, without which it would not be possible for him to dispose of even the small quantity of grain and vegetables which he cultivates. At an earlier period, I imagine that the breed must have been more like our Highland pony; but the government of France, with the view of improving the race, have established *Haras* in each of the departments. These Haras are well worth visiting, not so much from the character of the horses they contain, as from the care which is exhibited in the management of the establishment. In some of these stables there are above fifty stalls on a side, neatly divided and arranged. The ceiling is in general lofty, and a most perfect system of cleanliness pervades the whole. So many horses together, and so well kept, even although not remarkable for their beauty, form a sight to be admired. But notwithstanding the great expense attending these haras, (some of them costing above ten thousand pounds a year,) the benefit derived from them has been very inconsiderable.

In the breeding of horses, the French are very ignorant, for hitherto they seem to have imagined that the quality of the stock does not, in the least, depend on that of the dam. Consequently each peasant possessed of a half-starved disproportioned animal, brings her to the haras, and although the sire may be English, Norman, or Arabian, the progeny is very little, if at all better either in appearance or in usefulness than the mother. I am rather inclined to believe that the consequence has been to deteriorate the native breed, and to introduce a race of slight *weedy* creatures, infinitely worse adapted for burden than they must have been previous to the introduction of the haras. Besides, the peasant could not afford to keep a good horse until he could sell it to advantage. He has neither the means, nor the inclination, and it would not suit the purpose for-which he requires it; so that the only advantage which has hitherto been derived from these haras has been now and then obtaining a few horses for the cavalry. Thus the French, as well as the English, can boast of their sinecure and unprofitable establishments.

Horses, such as they are, are nowhere cheaper than in the neighbourhood of the Pyreneés; their prices ranging from two to five hundred francs. A few of the larger mares from which the peasants are in the habit of breeding mules, fetch the highest prices, but twenty pounds is in general considered a high price for a *cheval de pays*. At any of the great fairs of Pau, Tarbes, Oleron, &c., a very tolerable hackney may be procured for twelve or fifteen pounds; and as there are few of the gentlemen known in England as horse-dealers, to be met with at these places, it is not requisite that the purchaser should be a perfect connoisseur in horseflesh, in order to avoid being taken in. The peasant, in general, brings to market the horse which he wishes to dispose of, and the only rule to be observed in dealing with him, is invariably to offer him not more than one-half of what he demands at first;

for it seems to be an established custom with the peasantry, whenever they have any article to sell, to ask double its value; or rather, they expect the buyer to offer what he thinks its value, instead of their fixing the price themselves, and then abiding by it.

There is a great deal of amusement to be had at some of the great fairs, particularly at those held in the towns adjoining the Spanish frontier. There are then assembled together individuals from all parts of the two countries, dressed in their various costumes, speaking many different languages or dialects, and altogether dissimilar in appearance. But the erect, haughty, and in general, fine looking men from the Spanish side of the Pyreneés, will invariably be found the most interesting class. Some of these men are so very remarkable in their appearance, that frequently, in the midst of a fair, and when bargaining for a horse I have been elbowed by one of them, my attention has been withdrawn from my more immediate pursuit to contemplate a nobler creature, and to regret that so fine a people as the Spanish, should, by bad government and religious domination, be reduced to their present deplorable situation. The Spanish character is, as I have before observed, generally misunderstood, and too frequently belied. Those who declare them to be exclusively a haughty and vindictive people, seem to forget that they possess such qualities as gratitude for benefits, which no time nor change of circumstances can efface; and an anxiety to make amends, when they have acted or judged wrongly, which their eagerness to atone for by attentions and kind offices never fails of evincing. The Spanish character must not, as is almost always the case, be drawn from the manners and conduct of the nobility, in general a degraded class, altogether unworthy of their country, and as unlike its fine peasantry in personal appearance as they are inferior to them in the qualities of the mind and heart.

The number of mules exported from France to Spain, is immense. Several thousands of these animals may be seen at any of the great fairs, almost the whole of which are bought for the Spanish market. These mules are of various sizes and prices, and some of them very beautiful; their sires are the magnificent Spanish asses which are brought into France. The price of these mules depends upon their strength and size. A pair standing about sixteen hands in height, cannot be purchased for less than forty or fifty pounds. The females always sell considerably higher than the males, on account of their tractability; being much less obstinate, and performing their work more willingly. The strength and endurance of these fine animals (one or two of which are generally to be seen in the team of the heavy roulage, or carrier's carts) is prodigious; but the mules bred in France are intended for the Spanish market, and with the exception of the above instances, it is only the very inferior animals which are retained in the country. It is no unfrequent sight to witness upon the great road, a Spanish mule merchant, mounted on horseback, with fifty or a hundred of these animals, tied in pairs, trotting after him. The respectability of these Spanish merchants is so great, that they are trusted to any amount in France. This, considering the disturbed state of the country, and that no redress could be had, should they violate their engagements, is sufficient evidence as to their character.

There are annual horse-races at Tarbes, and

other of the Pyrenean towns, established by the government with a view to improving the breeds. I went to these races, expecting to find them much inferior to the worst *cock-tail* meetings at home; but, on the contrary, I found them wonderfully good, considering the little knowledge which the French have of the *science,* and the still less enthusiasm with which they indulge in it. So little do the people of the country care about beholding this sport, that they never, as in England, assemble in great numbers to witness it; in fact, it is altogether foreign to them. Horse-racing and fox-hunting are amusements which belong exclusively to England; the French never have distinguished themselves in either, and never can. Of their fox-hunting I shall now give an account *.

The vanity of the French—that ruling principle in their national character, which leads them to estimate every thing produced by their country as infinitely superior to every other — prevents them from adopting many of the comforts and substantial improvements which

---

* It may not be improper to mention, that a part of this chapter has already appeared in a periodical.

have been the results of experience and wisdom in other countries, and also from participating in the enjoyments of their more active and manly amusements. France is a large country, and in its many provinces there exists a wide and marked difference in the manners, language, and character of the inhabitants, amounting, in many instances, almost to a total dissimilarity; but throughout them all, this national vanity, this idea of superiority of intellect, this self-love and self-flattery, is inherent. It flourishes alike in the cold regions of the north, and in the more genial climate of the south; it is the one great and all-powerful chain which binds opposing parties and conflicting interests together, in every instance, and upon all occasions, where " La belle France," her honour, real or imaginary, is threatened with assault. They will uphold different political parties — they will aim at different forms of government—they will support a despotism, a mixed constitution, or a republic — a Louis Philippe, a Henry the fifth, or a Bonaparte—as it may suit their wavering and uncertain minds; and each and all of these factions will find, among the throng, partizans to shout the " vive " for them; but let the cry of " Vive la France !"

be raised, and, for the moment, all rivalry, all party animosity, will appear to cease; and the enthusiastic acclamations which rend the air, will tell a tale from whose moral each successive power that has ruled over the French nation for any length of time, has learned to gild the chains with which it fettered the people; and, by throwing around its acts the flimsy but effectual web of nationality, to unite under it all sects and parties, moulding them to its will. Thus it has been, and thus it will continue.

The church and the ancient aristocracy of France (which, but for their own narrow policy and consummate folly, might still have remained) are now gone; and each individual who aspires to wear the laurel-wreath entwined for him by the fickle fancy of the moment, must, if he wishes to retain it, bear well in mind the ruling foible of the people whom he would govern. Upon this as the only resting-place among the shoals and whirlpools which surround him, threatening him each moment with destruction, he must lay the foundation of all his actions; and he may, for a long, a very long period, rule over the most capricious nation on the face of the globe.

But what has all this moralizing to do with fox-hunting? Why, it has more than may at first appear; for, although the French do ape us in many matters, still their confounded vanity prevents them doing so to the letter; and, consequently, they bungle and destroy, where they might, were they less conceited, have become worthy and successful imitators—and so it is in *fox-hunting*.

The notions which the French have regarding this true English sport, are so very antiquated, that they are, in all probability, derived from some fox-hunting cavaliers who accompanied Charles the Second in his exile; for I imagine that it was before, or about that period, that their practices existed in England, if they were ever known there at any time.

Long ago, in England—

> " Our squires of old would rouse the day
> To the sound of the bugle horn;"

and, upon the same principle which led them to do so, I suppose the French act in the present day; and no arguments, no expostulations drawn from the practice in the land of fox-hunting, will induce them to alter or improve their mode of going to work. "It is not so in France," is the universal and conclusive answer. Thus, whoever wishes to go French fox-hunting, must make up his mind to tumble out of bed by half-past four, or five, at the latest. Should it rain while he is dressing, he may go to bed again, for, in their opinion, the scent will not lie at all; and should a shower or two fall in the course of the day, the faults and mistakes committed, whether on the part of the huntsmen or the dogs, are most knowingly laid to the account of the weather.

I have seen one or two dogs good enough to have held a respectable place, even in an English pack; but the generality are good for nothing. They never hunt with what we should call *courage*; but potter about like a parcel of pigs in an Indian corn field. Often have I been amused by observing some of them, when unable to pick up the scent, sit down on their hind quarters, and, with their noses in the air, composedly "bow-wow" away at the skies, instead of endeavouring to recover it, forgetting the new maxim of the politicians—*aide toi*. But one cannot, considering their training, blame them for this. In one particular, I think they are superior to our dogs, and that is, that their notes are even more musical; but this, I believe, is owing to the climate—for I have been informed that English dogs, after having been some time in France, acquire the same melody of sound. They are totally dissimilar in appearance: there is the heavy, strong, muscular animal, more adapted for a bear-hunt; the long-backed, greyhound-looking brute; and a cur, something like the beagle—in sweet confusion blended. The owner hunts them himself, and has a whipper-in, or "piqueur," as they call him, mounted; and sometimes another on foot. The hunting party must now be described; but they are sometimes so ludicrous in appearance, so oddly (at least to the eye of an Englishman) attired, mounted, and accoutred, that I fear I may fail in conveying a vivid impression of their appearance, which, indeed, beggars all description. To be justly appreciated, and sufficiently admired, it must be seen. Oh! what a despicable figure the gentlemen of any of our crack hunts would cut alongside of these worthies! Their heads are crowned with a three-cornered, 'fore-and-aft-looking cap of fur, of cloth, or of oil-cloth, with huge "fall downs" to cover the ears, and studded and illuminated all over with glittering steel buttons. A black stock, with a piece of whitish linen peeping over it, incloses the throat; and a green, dark brown, or velvet cut-away coat, and underneath it a bright crimson waistcoat, adorned with chains and clasps, and numberless odds and ends, and a broad leathern belt, drawn around their waists, dignify the upper man. Light coloured inexpressibles, of cloth or worsted cord, buttoned at the knee, or tied at the ankle; the enormous jack-boots of the Russian courier, or French gen-d'arme; or an imitation of our own hunting-boot, but substituting a polished leather top for the one which we prefer; with a pair of spurs, which, in length and size, would mock even those of our old moss-troopers—complete a costume which is neither to be met with nor equalled anywhere, save in France. I have also seen French officers turn out in full uniform, sword and altogether; and ladies with their horses' tails elegantly twisted in their cruppers, to preserve them from the mud.

The quality of their horses being of little consequence in their style of hunting, some are mounted upon nags of sixteen hands high; others upon what, in the Highlands of Scotland, are called "shelties." As to their saddles, some are demi-piques; some have, and some have not, cloaks or great coats fastened in front or behind, either to preserve them from the weather, or in their seats; a pair of holsters, (the most sensible part of the whole,) one containing a loaf of bread, and the other a flask of wine; and cruppers—that deformity to a horse, without which you seldom or never see a Frenchman ride. A few of the party frequently augment these incumbrances to their horses, by the addition of a "cutty gun."

There are generally two horns to a pack, the one carried by the owner, or a friend, the other by the piqueur. These instruments have a mouth of at least a foot and a half in diameter; and when not in use, are suspended in the same manner as our shot-belts, by thrusting the head and one arm through the centre of their coils.

In the neighbourhood of Pau, there is an immensity of the very finest cover. Both gorse and copse, in abundance, perhaps too much;

there is, therefore, no lack of foxes. One of the most frequent places of rendezvous for the pack which hunt the part of the country to which I particularly allude, is a place called the Bois de Pau. It is a wood, consisting of perhaps a couple of hundred acres, cut up and intersected in all directions by wide alleys and avenues. The French have no idea of a "run," their chief object being to accomplish what we call "mobbing in cover;" and this, to give them justice, they do set about in a most business-like manner. The dogs are thrown in a corner of this large wood, and instantly the hunters, like "knowing" old sportsmen in pheasant or woodcock shooting, gallop off to the different openings to guard them, and prevent Reynard, should he be inclined to break cover, and, if possible, to head him back into the woods; at the same time, never failing, if they have a gun, to salute him with a shot. A fox is generally found here, and after having been perhaps twenty or thirty times fired at and wounded, he is, in a short period, either most barbarously killed, or run to ground. Scampering up and down the alleys, or upon the road, and bawling and shouting, afford great amusement to the hunters; but of leaping, or going across the country, they are guiltless. The shots are frequently as likely to take effect upon some of the party as upon the ill-used fox; and one day, a cantonnier, at work upon the road, was all but struck by a ball fired in the wood.

Sometimes, when they run a fox to ground, they unearth him, and turn him out on some other day. Upon one occasion, they thus acquired as fine a fox as I ever saw; and we (the English) had some hopes of having a good day's sport with him. There is some very pretty country for riding across in the valley to the south-west of Pau, abounding in fences, but none of a very difficult nature; and we urged the master of the hounds to unbag him there; but our entreaties could not overcome their insurmountable objection to leaping, and the master resolved to turn him loose in the same place where he was found—their favourite haunt, the Bois de Pau. This fox was a fine catch for them; but not satisfied with admiring each other's feats of noisy brawl and hardy daring in the field, they were determined that the fair sex should have an opportunity of admiring their achievements. But, as all this took place during the carnival—the dancing and quadrilling period of the year among the French—it was some time before a day occurred upon which the ladies, sufficiently refreshed by a night's rest, could accompany their cavaliers to the chase. Thus the period of the imprisonment of this unfortunate victim, was lengthened out beyond the fortnight; during which time he was fed high, and put out of wind.

Secure of finding a fox, and their gallantry forbidding them to disturb the ladies at so early an hour as their usual time of starting, eleven o'clock was the hour fixed upon, and the everlasting wood the place of rendezvous. A friend and myself were among the last of leaving Pau, to join in the feats of this eventful day; and, in crossing the extensive *landes* which separate the town from the wood, we overtook the individual who, in a basket upon his head, was conveying the fox. Of course, we were much disgusted at the mode of proceeding, and I voted for upsetting the basket, and giving Reynard his liberty, at least a couple of miles from the wood, as he might, perhaps, take an opposite direction to it, and the hounds being brought and laid upon the scent, we, in all probability, would for once see something to bring home to our recollection. But my sagacious plan was overruled, and the man and his burden were allowed to proceed in the even tenor of their way.

Upon arriving at the wood, we found the assembled host, on "dreadful thoughts intent," waiting anxiously for the coming of the object of all their hopes and wishes. We pleaded hard that twenty or thirty minutes' *law* should be given him. But no; the hounds were to be slipped upon him the moment that he started. The basket was set down, and the lid lifted; when I observed that the fox was attached, by a chain, to the inside, (which would somewhat have deranged my plan of upsetting the basket upon the landes,) and he was so fierce that they could hardly untie it. To accomplish this, they let him get half way out of the basket, and then squeezing the lid down upon him, they, with less danger from his teeth, managed, after having, I have no doubt, broken at least two or three of his ribs, to give him his freedom.

But, to my astonishment, they had resolved to

make a dandy of him; and for that purpose, had adorned his neck with a huge collar, with loads of small bells attached to it. This was horrid! In fact, he only wanted the tea-canister to his tail, to complete his costume. The chain being unloosed, he went off in great style, his bells jingling like those of a posthorse; and, before he had made a hundred yards, away went the dogs after him. No sooner had the dogs started, than all the French party galloped off, not after them, but before them, leaving them to hunt in the best manner they could; forgetting, or unconscious, that the most beautiful and most *intellectual* part of a fox-hunt, is that, when the dogs, either having met with a check, display their sagacity and tact in recovering what the French call the "*quête*," and having succeeded, send forth the heart-stirring and joyous notes which tell us of the fact; or when, with their heads no longer at the earth, they sky along, breast high, causing the woods to ring again, and seeming to repeat the words of the old song—

"Follow who can—oh, then! oh, then!"

Breaking from the patch of wood to which he had made at first, he was headed, in the next alley, into another division; and thus it continued, for about twenty minutes, out of one square into another; until, at last, being driven into a corner and mobbed, he was either killed by the dogs, or frightened to death by the hubbub. I think the latter must have been the cause of his death; for, when I came up to the spot, I found him seemingly uninjured by the dogs: but at all events, he was, as the criers in the streets say, " most barbarously murdered." The body was then tied upon the pummel of the master's saddle, his head dangling upon one side, and his brush upon the other; so that passengers on either side of the road, or damsels gazing from the windows of the street, might not be deprived of a sight of the glorious trophy, nor ignorant of the prowess by which it had been acquired.

This was what the French call " *une grand chasse.*" As only one half of the wood had been disturbed, the remainder was " drawn " for another fox: but without success. The owner of the pack, upon this, observed to me, " that it was no use drawing any more covers, as there had been rain in the morning." I thought of the " Fox and the Grapes," and said that, in England, frequently, the very best runs took place on rainy days; and, not only was such the case, but I had more than once had my red coat made white with snow upon days on which I had seen very fair sport. "*Mon Dieu! mais c'est tout à fait different en France.*"

The hounds of Tarbes are much better, and the owner takes considerable interest in them. He has a court-yard behind his house, along one side of which is a double range of berths, each large enough for two dogs, and in which his hounds are kept exceedingly dry and clean. M. Dupont, the proprietor, who is a very polite person, frequently invites the English at Pau to come and have a few days' hunting with him; and, what is rather unusual for a Frenchman, he never fails to give them one or two most excellent dinners.

Wolf and hare hunting are his favourite amusements; for, although to oblige us he would sometimes hunt a fox, still he is averse to it; as he thinks that the scent of the fox being so much ranker than that of the wolf, it spoils the dogs for the latter sport. I was not so fortunate as to be present at a wolf-hunt with his hounds.

The wolves are frequently driven down from the mountains by the snow, and take refuge in the woods of the low country; and the peasants, when they see them there, inform M. Dupont of their presence. The wolf is a more difficult customer to deal with than the fox. He is hardly ever killed by being fairly run down by the dogs. Very few instances of wolves being so killed are known; although runs of this kind have been known to last a day and a night—the dogs following the same wolf for that length of time. On this account, the hunters always endeavour to wound or cripple him, so as to put him upon a more *equal footing* with the dogs; and, accordingly, every one, upon such occasions, is armed. Even when wounded, the wolf, if he is a strong one, will hold on for three or four hours; during which time, both dogs and horses, if their riders will follow, will have had enough of it. Oh! that I could see a first-rate pack of English dogs laid upon a wolf's track! It would, indeed, be a sight worth seeing. He would find an enemy worth contending with; one that would not permit him,—as is frequently the case,—when having gained upon his pursuers, and aware of his superiority over them, to rest himself composedly until they come up, and then start off, as fast and as fresh as ever; but, that would hang heavy on his heels, not quit him until their strength failed them, or they had him in their fangs. It would be a glorious sight!

But, to return to M. Dupont's hounds. Afraid that we should not get out of bed early enough, M. Dupont had ordered his piqueur to come to our hotel about four in the morning, and "blow us up" with his great horn. About five, the master and his hounds, and a party of French gentlemen arrived, and we, being all ready, joined them. There were symptoms of rain; and, in the dusk of the morning, each of our companions being enveloped in a waterproof cloak, or great coat, the assemblage looked more like a detachment of monks going to a funeral than a party of jovial hunters. Our master of the hounds, a most enormous man, could not, with jack-boots, great coat, blunderbuss, holsters and all, ride under one and twenty stone. He was mounted upon a small chestnut mare, with legs like those of an elephant, and it was amazing to see how she moved under the prodigious weight she carried.

In hare-hunting, they have a tolerably good reason for disturbing one's sleep so early in the morning. There are (as every peasant carries a gun, and every man and boy in the whole country spend half their time in shooting) very few hares, and, consequently, the difficulty of finding them in their forms is very great. To obviate this, they endeavour either to come upon puss when she is actually feeding; or, if too late for that, skirting all the spots where she has been likely to do so, to come upon her scent, and track her to her form. This is a very good plan, if pursued soon after she has been feeding, but it will not do any length of time after she has gone; and, of course, if a hare is not found before eight or nine in the morning, she will not, in all probability, be found at all. Hare-hunting is not worth describing, because every body knows what it is, and few people care for it. But the scene which took place upon our return home was too laughable to be passed over.

Before entering the town, we were requested

to ride in a body; and the day having become fine, great coats and cloaks were all doffed, and strapped to the saddle-bows. Our companions, of whom during the day we had seen nothing but their faces, were now transformed into exquisites of the first water: and so completely indeed had they protected themselves from the rain and mud, that they looked more as if they had just finished their toilet than been exposed to the annoyances of ploughed fields and splashing roads. As for us, we resembled a parcel of half drowned rats, who would willingly have sneaked into their holes to avoid the vulgar gaze which the presence of such gay cavaliers could not fail to attract; but, as we were told that our leaving the troop might be thought disrespectful to the master, we courageously faced the approaching exhibition. There are,—as I observed before,—generally, two of these abominable French horns in a hunting party, the one carried by the piqueur, the other by the master, or a friend. M. Dupont's nephew was the bearer of this—to the ears of a sportsman—most disagreeable instrument; and he rode at the head of the party: while the piqueur, with the dogs and the other horn, brought up the rear. In this manner, we rode into the town of Tarbes, our leader halting at each turn or winding of the streets, and sounding the "*Tantara*" for a few seconds; after he had been answered by the piqueur, with the other horn, from the rear, he moved on again, thus giving warning of our approach, and affording all the inhabitants plenty of time to come to their windows, and admire us. Glad were we, when the neighbourhood of our hotel permitted us to escape.

CHAPTER XX.

Superstitions of the Bearnais, and Haute Pyrenean Peasantry—Remnants of Ancient Mythology—Zeal in celebrating their Religious Ceremonies—Pilgrimages—Disregard of the Decrees which abolished Religion—Character of the Inhabitants of Bearn—Ancient Laws of their Country—Dislike of the new Laws of Division—Various Superstitions of the Mountaineers—Ceremonies at their Marriages—Superstitions of the Roussillon Peasantry—Celebration of the Mysteries—Processions of the Flagellans—Processions of the Semaine Sainte—Poetry and Music of the Pyreneés.

In the Pyrenean departments,—into whose mountain districts civilization progresses with but slow and tardy steps,—the manners and customs of the people are but little altered from what they were centuries ago. In the neighbourhood, indeed, of the watering-places, the tastes and the habits of the peasantry are fast changing; and there, the greed of gain drying up the springs of their native kindliness and generosity, the stranger is only welcomed according to the price which he can pay for his entertainment. But, away from these emporia of demi-Parisien vice, the Pyrenean peasantry still retain their pristine simplicity, religious feelings, and hospitality. In the humble cabin of the shepherd will be found many traces of the olden times; and, in the superstitions of its inhabitants, remnants of the mythology of the earliest periods, mingled with the fables and customs of the middle ages; and, left in a great degree stationary, although in the vicinity of civilization, they have preserved their virtues, their customs, and their traditions.

Excepting in a few valleys in the mountains of the Basque country, where Protestantism prevails, the inhabitants of the Pyreneés are Roman Catholics. No people are more attached to their sacred rites; and they solemnize, with zeal, the great religious festivals, and practise with much care the lesser observances of their creed. If, during a market, during the labours of the field, in the midst of the most animated rejoicings, or of their favourite dances, the bell of the neighbouring hamlet announces the hour of prayer, the traveller stops, the labourer abandons his spade or his plough, the rejoicings, the dances cease, and every one kneeling down, they offer up their prayers.

Threatened by the tempest, the sailor from the shores of Aquitaine, Languedoc, or Provence, turns his thoughts to his village altars, and implores the Virgin to intercede for him, and restore him to his parents, or his wife and children. The most pompous of the Catholic ceremonies delight the people of the Pyreneés, and the longest and most fatiguing pilgrimages are made in order to be present at them. I have already taken notice of the "Fete de la Vierge" held at Betharam, whose chapel and *Calvaire* are the most celebrated throughout Guienne, and to which the peasantry of Béarn and Bigorre, upon the eighth of September, may be seen to the number of many thousands, wending their way. I have also noticed the pilgrimages to the lonely chapel in the wild valley of Héas, and those to St. Bertrand, which last are not only attended by the inhabitants of the surrounding country, but by hundreds from the Spanish valleys.

The inhabitants of the Pyreneés, favoured by their situation, and their distance from the metropolis, and induced by their religious zeal, paid little regard to the decrees of the Revolutionists forbidding the observance of religion throughout the empire; but, comparatively safe from persecution in their mountain fastnesses, supported their pastors in their religious administration, and bade defiance to the authority of the commissioners sent to shut up their churches, and punish them for their contumacy.

The character of the Bearnais peasantry is exceedingly well portrayed by M. du Mège. He says—" Les Béarnais ont un caractère qui rassemble à celui des peuples qui les environnent : ils sont en général fins, dissimulés, méfians, intéressés, envieux, irascibles, et jaloux de leur liberté. C'est un peuple spirituel, propre à tout ce qui demande de l'intelligence et de la souplesse, et dans lequel on remarque un air de fierté, de civilisation et de politesse, qu'on ne voit point ailleurs. Dans les vallées, il a l'esprit plus delié, et un physique plus robuste ; il tient à sa religion, sans être fanatique ni intolérant. Le deployement de la puissance l' étonne peu ; mais il est naturellement soumis aux loix. Son orgueil et son irascibilité le portent facilement à la vengeance ; mais, contenu par la crainte de la fletrissure et de la perte de son bien, il fait éclater son ressentiment par les moyens judiciares. Lorsqu' il est vaincu, il est plus humilié du triomphe de son adversaire, que sensible au dommage qu' il éprouve : nulle partie du Departement ne donne autant d'occupation aux tribunaux.

"Les mœurs des Béarnais sont douces, même celles des habitans des montagnes, lesquels, forcés par les neiges de descendre, et de passer l'hiver avec leurs troupeaux dans le plat pays, s'y policent, et perdent leur rudesse naturelle. Rarement des crimes atroces déshonorent les habitans de cette contrée : les rixes des cabarets, la violation des règlemens ruraux et forestiers, y sont les délits les plus fréquens."

There are many causes which have contributed to form the character of this interesting people. Their ancient constitution was singularly favourable to liberty, compared to that of the people of the interior. The early division of the soil rendered nearly the whole of the population labouring proprietors; and, even now-a-days there is scarcely any one who cultivates another's land; and, in almost every instance where additional labourers are required by the proprietors of the larger vineyards, the individuals employed are the Spaniards, from the frontier provinces who emigrate to France in search of work. No wonder that the Bearnais peasantry are a joyous race, and the burdens of life hang lightly upon their shoulders; they are the cultivators of their own land, and they know that *they* alone will reap its fruits.

The order of succession established by the ancient laws of the country, and which perpetuated the comfort of the families, by preserving their paternal acres, although limited, secured to the industrious cultivator a competence, and preserved his independence. The climate also influences in a great degree the character of the Bearnais; its mildness aids him in his labours, while its steadiness, giving him confidence that they will be repaid, renders him cheerful and contented.

The laws of Bearn, remarkable for their wisdom, founded upon the respect of persons and of property, contain many maxims of the purest morality. They were very favourable to paternal authority. They obliged a son, living in comfort, to maintain his father, if he was poor. They desired a father to settle in marriage his daughters, in preference to his sons, and dispensed with his endowing a child who had wandered from the paths of virtue. They reprobated idleness as the mother of vice, and they punished very severely those who were guilty of perjury, deceit, usury, theft, and other crimes. There is also a law which does much honour to the Bearnais; it regards the great respect paid to females in child-bed. They prohibited any seizure being made in a house during their confinement, and until ten days after the birth of their children. No nation was more aware of the truth of the maxim, that good laws insure good manners.

Each individual was at full liberty to dispose of those goods which he had himself acquired; but lands acquired by succession were unalienable but by the third generation. They could not be sold without the authority of the judge, and but from absolute necessity, and even then only the fourth part could be sold.. The right of primogeniture was in full force; but, at the same time, there were certain provisions for the younger children. The natural effect of this arrangement was, that the eldest son, aware of the rights of his brothers and sisters, and that, in the absence of funds to pay their portions, the burden would fall upon the estate to which he would succeed, wrought hard during the lifetime of his father, and saved money to pay off the family provisions. These provisions enabled the females to contract suitable marriages with heirs of a fortune almost equal to that of their brother. The younger sons, on the other hand, married heiresses, who brought to them not only their provisions, but the sums which their father or brother had given them, to induce them to work at home until their marriage. These provisions generally consisted of a certain number of cattle bred among the herds of their father or brother.

Such were the ancient laws of the country; to which the inhabitants are still so very much attached, that, in general, the fathers, by means of fictitious sales, convey the property to their eldest sons; and, in a great number of families, the younger sons never avail themselves of the advantages bestowed upon them by the new laws of division. In the Basque country, in particular, the peasant preserves, with a sort of religious veneration, the patrimony of his fathers.

The successive political revolutions have not effaced the superstitions and customs of the early ages. The fountains, the lakes, the rivers, are still in some degree the objects of veneration to the inhabitants of these provinces, who throw into their waters pieces of silver, of food, and of raiment.

On the eve of St. John, they wash with the dew their eyes, or other parts of their bodies, weakened by infirmities; and those who have any disease of the skin, roll themselves among the heaps of corn wet with it.

They bestow the name of *Loup-Garou* on a most changeable spirit who appears in various forms, sometimes as a dog, remarkable for its whiteness, at the spot where four roads meet; sometimes dragging chains, the echo of which is heard at great distances.

"Do you wish for the riches of this world?" say the Bearnais, "pay your homage to the fairy who resides in a cavern beneath the oak of Escout: there deposit a purse, invoke the Supreme Arbiter of your destinies, and retire. Return in a few hours afterwards, and you will find your purse full of gold and silver." They even point out persons who have acquired their fortunes in this manner.

They are also acquainted with the ceremonies practised by the Druids, in regard to certain plants. If an infant is attacked by a fever, his nurse, believing that medical aid will be fruitless, invokes a stalk of wild mint as the divinity who can succour her; to it she makes an offering of bread covered with salt, and, addressing it in rhyme, repeats the ceremony nine times. The plant dies; and the child is cured.

They also believe, that, by carrying certain sacred plants about them, they are preserved from every evil.

Fennel is, among the Bearnais, the plant whose kindly influence is a protection against evil spirits. I recollect a peasant pointing out to me a variegated leaf, the spots upon which he declared had been caused by some drops of the

Virgin's milk which had been spilt upon them while suckling our Saviour.

Sarrante is consecrated to the Virgin; the faithful who go there to offer up their devotions, bring back a piece of the rock. The same custom is common in the valley of Héas, where each pilgrim carries away a fragment of the "Caillou d' Araye."

They draw inferences, lucky or unlucky, from the songs and flights of birds, or the howling of dogs.

When they hear the cry of the screech-owl they fear a misfortune; the peasants then throw salt into the fire to prevent the accomplishment of the threatened evil.

If a magpie while chattering looks at you, or turns towards your habitation, you ought to hope for something lucky; but, if it crosses your path, or flies to your left hand, it predicts evil.

The number thirteen is unlucky. There are persons who will not sit down to a table with thirteen guests. The number three is lucky.

At the entrance to the valley d' Aspe may be seen a large conical stone; "les femmes vont y frotter leur ventre, quand elles sont frappées de stérilité."

The birth of a child is the occasion of many ceremonies. The moment it is born they throw out of the window corn, or pieces of money; and, when the infant is carried to the baptismal fount, they place upon him a morsel of bread, which is given to the first person they meet.

When a marriage takes place, the companions of the bridegroom are called *donzelous*, the friends of the bride *donzelles*. The bride is conducted with great pomp to the house of her husband, generally preceded by a lamb adorned with streamers; and nuptial songs are sung. The procession stops at a little distance from the house of the husband, and a party is sent forward to treat with the father-in-law. Soon after, the procession moves on, and arrives at its destination. The nuptial songs are redoubled; corn and other fruits—tokens of abundance—are thrown in at the windows; the doors are opened, and, in the midst of joyous shouts, the wedding-cake, carried by the friends of the husband, is divided among the relations and friends of the bride.

In some parts of the Hautes Pyreneés there exist confused recollections of the fables of the middle ages. The fairies, *Hados*, strange beings, called also sometimes, *las Blanquettes*, occupy a conspicuous place in the popular superstitions. The peasant believes that they are sometimes seen dancing by the mysterious light of the moon, sometimes upon the summits of the mountains, sometimes upon the ancient towers, or in the verdant meadows. Flowers spring up where their feet have pressed the sward; they increase or diminish the storms at their will; and shower down benefits upon those who render them sincere homage. Some of them inhabit the interior of the Pic de Bergons, and change, in an instant, into the finest thread the flax which has been left at the entrance of their solitary abode. In the valley of Barousse (the least known, perhaps, of all the Pyrenean valleys) during the night which precedes the first day of the year, the fairies enter the houses of their devotees. They bring happiness in their right hand, in the form of an infant crowned with flowers, and misfortune in their left, represented by another infant, who weeps. The peasantry have been careful to prepare in a clean and empty chamber, the repast which they wish to offer their guests. A white cloth covers the table upon which is placed a loaf, a knife, a jug of water, or of wine, with a cup and a candle in the midst. They believe that those who offer the best food, may hope to have their herds increased, their harvests abundant, and that marriage will crown their dearest hopes; but those who fail in these attentions to the fairies, and who neglect to make preparations worthy of the spirits who come to visit them, may expect the greatest misfortunes; fire will consume their dwellings, wild animals devour their flocks, hail will destroy their harvests, or their infants die in the cradle. Upon the first day of the year, the father, the eldest person, or the master of each house, takes the bread which has been offered to the fairies, breaks it, and after having dipped it in the water or the wine, contained in the jug, distributes it among the family, and also among the servants; after this they wish each other a good year, and breakfast upon the bread.

The peasantry on the banks of the Garonne suppose that the inundations of the river are occasioned by wicked spirits bathing in its springs; and blame them as the cause of the rains and thunder-storms. When the late but abundant harvests of the valleys are suddenly destroyed, *l' Homme Noir*, an evil genius, is seen hovering upon the summit of a neighbouring peak, shaking from his immense wings the hailstones which have blighted the labourer's hopes.

When a flower is seen to bloom among barren rocks, in places destitute of all other vegetation, it is in general thought a certain omen of an abundant harvest throughout the country. When a tree spreads its branches over the roof of a house, it is believed to predict all kinds of misfortunes to its inhabitants; that the sons will die in distant lands; that the mother will not find comfort in her daughters; and the father, forsaken by his children, and abandoned by his friends, will live to old age in wretchedness and poverty.

Many omens are drawn from flowers. When a rose is left alone upon its thorny stalk, and when it bends towards a house, it predicts the death of one of the inhabitants.

There are many curious ceremonies to be witnessed at marriages and births. In the commune of Massat the bride breaks away from the procession conducting her to her husband's abode, and flies for refuge to a house which her companions, armed with swords, undertake to defend (these girls are called *espaseros*, from the weapons which they carry); soon after, the companions of the bridegroom, armed in the same manner, come and besiege the house, and after a suitable resistance, the *espaseros* yield, and the besiegers carry off the bride in triumph.

But one of the most beautiful sights to be beheld in the south, is the illumination which takes place on the eve of St. John. Every height is then crowned with fires; hundreds of them may be seen at the same instant, and the whole country appears in one blaze of light.

The mountaineers, as I have mentioned in a former chapter, pay great respect to the fountains; they even make offerings to them; and, in some districts, when the snows have melted, they assemble at the first appearance of the morning star, and climbing to the top of a hill, place themselves in a circle, and wait in silence for the rising of the sun; as soon as it has appeared, the most aged of the group begins to pray, while the others attend in silence. After having prayed, the shepherds allot the pasturages and cabins, and separating, form their colonies; each colony elects its chief, (a dignity invariably bestowed upon hoary locks,) who bears the name of *le père, le vieux;* then the chiefs, assembling together, swear to love God, to render assistance to travellers and wanderers, and to offer them milk and fire, and the use of their cloaks and cabins: to reverence the fountains, and to take care of the flocks.

The superstitious observances which I have now related, are but a tithe of those which exist in the central and western departments of the Pyreneés. In Roussillon, where the people are entirely Roman Catholics, and far more Spanish than French in their manners and character, the remnants of the old religious ceremonies and sacred rites are more frequent in their occurrence, and more perfect in their observance. The most interesting and remarkable of these ceremonies are the dramatic representations, called *Mysteries;* and which, practised very generally throughout Europe at one period, and now succeeded by our modern drama, are still extant in Roussillon and part of Spain. These religious theatricals are performed in the language of the department. The legend of the patron saint, to which the parish church is dedicated, usually forms the subject of the piece; at other times it is taken from the Bible. *La Presa del Hort*, (the capture in the garden,) is one of the most common; the play begins with the creation, and concludes with the death of our Saviour. The costumes of the actors are most ridiculous, and it is by no means uncommon to see a black-bearded man performing one of the female characters. The theatre is generally raised in the *place*, and in character and comforts very much resembles those of our strolling players. Planks resting upon chairs, tables, or benches, form the seats for the vulgar audience; while the aristocracy of the place, at the expense of a few *sous*, are accommodated with seats upon a higher platform. M. Henry gives a curious description of these Roussillon theatricals, in his observations upon the *Mystère de Sainte Basilice, et de Sainte Julien;* he represents to us the Saint Felicio dressed in a coat of changing colours above an embroidered vest of such length as nearly to cover his thighs, with white silk stockings, gold buckles, and his hair powdered; which, says M. Henry, "sous la main du perruquier, avoient pris un certain air de frisure, étoient légérement couverts de poudre; je dis légérement, et ce n' est pas sans intention, puisque ce fut par convenance que le coiffeur n'en mit pas davantage; en effet, quelqu' un lui ayant demandé pourquoi il ne poudrait pas complètement Felicio, il lui répondit d'un air capable: Ne voyez-vous pas que c'est un *Romain?* Notre Romain, donc, en père noble, et en habit gorge de pigeon, n' avoit pas oublié la canne à pomme d' or, et il en faisait un usage fort indiscret, car il ne manquait pas d' en frapper le plancher à la fin de chaque *hémistiche;* en sorte que toutes les fois qu'il se trouvait en scène avec le père de Sainte Basilice et l' oncle de Saint Julien, qui en avoient aussi chacun une, leur déclamation étoit accompagnée d'un certain bruit cadencé, qui ne resembloit pas mal à celui que font les forgerons."

"Felicia, la femme de Felicio dans la pièce, et son gendre hors de là, étoit un gros gaillard de cinq pieds cinq a six pouces, d'une robuste corpulence, et d'un teint brun fortement prononcé:

son costume consistait en une robe de damas jaune à grands ramages, de celles que portaient nos grand mères, ayant la queue, non pas retroussée par les coins, passée à travers l'ouverture des poches, mais pendante, car la taille du personage m' empêche de la dire traînante. Son col était emboîté dans une colerette à grands canons, et sur sa poitrine velue brillait une longue chaîne d'or; des pendeloques à la Catalane, c' est-à-dire, descendant jusqu' aux épaules, tenaient à ses oreilles, et ses cheveux frisés, et copieusement poudrés, malgré sa qualité de Romaine, étaient surmontés d'un diadème de carton couvert de papier doré. Pour adoucir le teint de sa peau, on avait chargé ses joues d'une forte couche de rouge de cinabar, en sorte que l'ensemble était d'un effet difficile à imaginer."

Before the Revolution, there were annual processions, the members of which were called *flagellans*, from the manner in which they beat themselves; half naked, and covered with blood, they ran about the streets, lacerating their bodies with whips, or cords with small bullets or pieces of iron attached to them. Towards the end of the last century the clergy and magistrates of the province wished to abolish these over-zealous exhibitions; but the force of custom prevailing, these processions were, after a short time, again renewed. In the early times of the Revolution, when the links of society were broken, and all authority disregarded, these frantic scenes were renewed to an excess which had never before been witnessed; numbers of *flagellans* took a part in all the processions; and what was still more extraordinary, each company of the National Guards had its own particular *flagellan*, who followed his comrades in uniform, with his taper in his hand. The dress of the *flagellan* consisted of fine white cloth, with flounces trimmed with black ribbon or lace; a large opening was left at the back of this dress, ornamented with gay ribbons; and a huge hood, four or five feet in height, was kept upright upon the head by a cone of pasteboard; upon the feet were worn white sandals embroidered with black, and in the right hand the *flagellan* held a whip formed of little cords, at the extremities of which were attached small pieces of iron or sharp-pointed silver stars, at each stroke of which the blood sprung from the body of the penitent. To make the blood flow plentifully; care was taken to rub with warm towels the parts which were to be struck, in order to heat the skin, and draw the blood towards it. Slight punctures were then made with the point of a lancet, so that the wounds, when struck, might bleed abundantly.

There is one other singular ceremony in Roussillon, which is practised during the last two nights of the *Semaine-sainte*, which considerably astonishes strangers. Processions are formed of numbers of men dressed in black gowns, tucked up with a white cotton cord, to which is attached an enormous rosary, with hoods on their heads like those of the *flagellans;* each of these penitents carries a taper, and they are arranged in two files, which the *regidors*, or masters of the ceremonies keep in order. In front of the procession is borne a banner of black damask, fringed with silver, and surmounted by a cross; two smaller banners, also black, are carried, upon which are represented the various symbols of the Passion; and at intervals, figures nearly as large as life, emblematical of the sufferings of our Saviour. In the centre of the lines of penitents, are children, also clad in black, and bearing little banners of silk embroidered in silver. To these are added a Roman centurion, accompanied by his soldiers (called *estafermes* in Catalan) supporting a standard with the four letters S. P. Q. R. *(Senatus Populus que Romanus)* embroidered upon it; and the priests of the different churches in their surplices, carrying tapers; this extraordinary assemblage is rendered still more grotesque by having players on bassoons among their ranks, and four or five violin players following the priests. Some idea of the procession upon the first night may be formed from this description.

Upon the second, they carry a cross of such large dimensions and great weight, that in order to preserve its equilibrium, they are obliged to walk very slow. The privilege of carrying this crucifix is eagerly contested; he who obtains this honour, must needs be of more than ordinary strength, or he will very soon resign it; the smallest stumble is sufficient to throw the cross from its equilibrium, and in falling, wound those in its neighbourhood. Upon this occasion, they also carry the tomb of Jesus Christ, upon the upper part of which, the Saviour is represented as dead, and lying in a bed, the coverlet of which is generally of crimson velvet, enriched with tassels and fringes of gold; the sheets are composed of the finest linen, and the pillows trimmed with lace. Formerly the ornaments of these processions were of Gothic workmanship, now they are entirely changed, and modern taste has introduced the designs of the different objects displayed in these nocturnal exhibitions.

These ceremonies, although somewhat grotesque, are still exceedingly striking to one who for the first time beholds them. The slow march of the extraordinarily dressed groups, indistinctly seen by the light of the tapers, and a few torches which accompany them, the dark masses of the spectators, and the waving branches of cypress which they carry, render the spectacle sufficiently imposing.

The mountains have generally been the asylum of the Muses; and nowhere have they been more favourably received than in the Pyreneés. Each district can boast of its native poets, and its peculiar songs, many of them remarkable for their beautiful simplicity and depth of feeling. Cradled among scenes of the wildest beauty, within hearing of the avalanches, the whooping of the eagles, and the roaring cataracts, it would be strange indeed, if the imagination of those so situated were not excited, and poetry did not flourish, where nature has done so much to engender it. The productions of the Pyrenean shepherds, far less known than they merit, have proved their country to have been a

"Meet nurse for a poetic child,"

and that while watching their flocks during the heats of the day, and the silence of the night, they have not been insensible to the objects around them—but in the solitude of the lonely cabin, they could give vent to their feelings in strains full of passion and tenderness. The subjects of their lays are most frequently the faithlessness of their mistresses, the love of their country, the death of one of their flocks, or other simple, but to them affecting incidents. These give birth to their effusions, which, although often irregular in their style, are not the less beautiful and interesting; and they only require a man of genius—a Walter Scott—well read in the traditionary lore of the mountains, to collect and arrange them, in order to render them most acceptable to the public.

The airs of the Pyreneés are not less remarkable for their beauty than for their spirit. Many celebrated composers have acquired fame, and in the theatres of the capital been applauded as the authors of airs of Pyrenean origin. Garat, the famous singer, in particular, had often recourse to the music of Roussillon to charm his auditors; but, well aware that in France, nothing would be acceptable without a foreign recommendation, he had the precaution to set Italian words to the music which he received from Perpignan; and those airs were then admired at Paris as the production of the virtuosos of Milan, of Rome, or of Naples, whose author had died unknown among the Pyreneés.

CHAPTER XXI.

Valley of the Neiss—Its great Beauty—Source of the Neiss—Valley d'Ossau—Marble Pillars in the Church of Bielle, and Anecdote of Henri IV.—Laruns—Route to Eaux Bonnes—Village of Eaux Bonnes, and Mineral Springs—Its Environs—Hunters of the Valley d'Ossau—Fine Appearance and good Character of its Peasantry—Best Period for Hunting in the Pyreneés—Izard and Bear Hunting—Narrow Escape of a Friend on a Hunting Excursion—Unsatisfactory Pursuit of a Bear and Cubs—Fonda, " le père des Chasseurs de la Valleé d'Ossau "—Appearance and character of the Man—Stalking of an Izard—Results—Driving of a Herd of Izards—Result—Presence of Mind of Pyrenean Hunters—Numerous Herds of Izards—Valley of Sousouel—Construction of a Hut—Arrival of our Provisions—Fonda's Adventures, and Death-bed Scene of his Father.

THE beautiful little valley of the Neiss opens immediately to the south of the town of Pau, and along the banks of its stream is the road to the watering-places of the Eaux Bonnes and the

Eaux Chaudes. Of all the valleys in this district, that of the Neiss is the largest; its scenery of woody dells and vine-clad hills is the most pleasing and varied; and the gorgeous views of the mountains, which are seen from many parts of it, the most striking and interesting. Leaving the village of Jurançon on the right,—where, under the shade of the great oak-trees which separate it from the road, the ever joyous Bearnais peasantry may be seen " tripping it lightly" upon Sundays and holidays,—the road crosses the bridge over the Neiss, and enters the valley.

The road for the first few miles is so perfectly straight, and bordered by Lombardy poplars of prodigious height, that it appears to be an avenue of most imposing grandeur, of which the termination is the gigantic forked peak of the Pic du Midi d' Ossau; which, conspicuous by its situation, and its peculiarity of form, is among the many objects which here draw the attention of the stranger, that of the most absorbing interest. Here the most extreme fertility prevails; Indian corn, the staple produce of the soil of Bearn, flourishes in the fields by the river-side; chateaux and farm-houses, surrounded by their vineyards and copses, hang upon the low hills which skirt the valley; and hundreds of little valleys, or rather glens, stretching away upon both sides, in whose secluded nooks the white-washed cottages of the peasant proprietor, half-hid among their fruit trees and vines, seem placed so as to overlook his little domain, add greatly to the rich-looking and delightful appearance of the valley. A few miles beyond the village of Gan, the valley narrows so much as to leave scarce sufficient space for the river and the road, and assumes the character of what in the Highlands of Scotland, would be called a *pass;* the resemblance to which is much increased by the quantity of heath which on every side displays its purple flowers.

At the village of Rebenac, the road again crosses the river, and begins to ascend the ridge which separates the valley of the Neiss from the valley d' Ossau. Before arriving at the summit may be seen the source of the Neiss, which, like many other rivers of the Pyreneés, bursts forth at once into a considerable stream from a cavern in the limestone rock. After crossing this ridge, the road winds along the banks of the Gave d'Ossau. The green and wooded hills of the Basque country are seen bounding to the west the rich plains of Arudy; and, at the picturesque little village of Louvie, we enter the valley d'Ossau, and become enclosed among the mountains which on either side hem in the valley. Here, as in the valleys of the Lavedan, the excellence of the climate permits the inhabitants of the mountains to cultivate their little patches of grain, at elevations where, in other countries, the heath or the fir would scarcely be able to struggle with the blasts; and villages, hamlets, and solitary chapels, are scattered among the slopes and shelves of the mountains.

In this valley, there are quarries of white marble, which, in early times, were wrought to a great extent. In the church of the village of Bielle, the altar is surmounted by four columns of the native marble. These columns were esteemed so highly by Henry IV. that, when adorning his chapel of the Louvre, he sent to request the inhabitants to present them to him. The answer returned to his Majesty was somewhat singular. "Sire," said they, " you are the master of our hearts and of our fortunes; but with regard to the columns of the temple, they belong to God: demand them from Him."

At Laruns, the roads to the Eaux Bonnes and the Eaux Chaudes separate; the former following the windings of the stream called the Valentine; the latter, ascending the mountain to the magnificent *pass* of the Hourat.

The road to the Eaux Bonnes has only within late years become safe and practicable for carriages of every description. Like that to Luz and Barèges, its formation has been a work of great labour and expense, turning and winding along the banks and precipices, sometimes embowered in wood, sometimes scooped out of the solid rock, or built along its ledges, where the river may be seen tossing through its rocky channel hundreds of feet below, or dashing over the numerous cascades in which its course abounds.

Of the village of Eaux Bonnes no traces are visible until we are close upon it; and the fine road which we are passing along, at every bend of which we expect to see the houses of the watering-place, becomes gradually so labyrinthed among the surrounding and overhanging precipices and mountains, that we begin to despair of the existence of any habitable dwelling-place, and imagine ourselves winding our way into the heart of the Pyrenean range, when a turn round a projecting crag discloses the little basin in which the houses and baths of the Eaux Bonnes are built. A more picturesque or extraordinary situation cannot be imagined than that of this watering-place; it is, as it were, engulfed among the mountains, whose precipices in many places form a part of the walls of its houses, and in others have been blasted in order to gain sufficient space to erect them.

The mineral waters are held in great estimation; and numbers annually arrive from all parts of France who hope to benefit by their medicinal properties, which first acquired their fame from the cures which they effected upon the wounded of the Bearnais soldiers whom Henri d' Albret led to the battle of Pavia. At that period, the waters were styled les Eaux des Arquebusades.

So hemmed in and inclosed, Eaux Bonnes, to the unfortunate who comes thither for the recovery of his health, must be a dreary place of sojourn, even in fine weather; in bad, I should think, almost insupportable: while, to those who have only amusement to entice them to its seclusion, and whose constitution will permit them to seek for health among the wild mountain scenery in its neighbourhood, — where the izard (the chamois of the Pyreneés) abounds, and the bear is not unfrequently to be met with,—it will, on the contrary, prove most attractive. Thus it was with myself, during the period when I resided in the vicinity of Pau; and the Eaux Bonnes was the head-quarters from which most of my shooting excursions in the Pyreneés were undertaken.

The chasseurs of the valley d'Ossau are justly considered among the most active and hardy in the mountains; and retain (with the few exceptions which the influx of strangers has occasioned) their native simplicity of manners and honesty of character. In appearance, there is no other valley of the Pyreneés whose inhabitants can compete with them; indeed, both the men and women of the valley d'Ossau are remarkable for the regularity of their features and handsome persons, which their original and most picturesque looking costumes render still more striking; and so kind and obliging, and free from prejudice are they, that the wanderer in their mountains is not only certain of being well received by them, but the shelter of their cabin, and a share of their humble fare he will invariably have proffered to him, and his acceptance esteemed a favour. The cursory observer, who may have been cheated by some of the idle individuals who, at the various watering-places, are ever on the alert to impose upon the credulity of visitors, would sadly mistake the character of the Pyrenean peasantry, were he to suppose that such conduct is general; on the contrary, the more I have mixed among them the better I have liked them, and the higher has my opinion of them risen.

The early part of the season, and before the snows have so completely melted as to permit the sheep and cattle to return to the high pastures, is the most favourable period for hunting the izard and bear. The haunts of those animals are then undisturbed by the shepherds and their dogs; the izards are most frequently found in herds, and are less timorous, while there still remains a sufficient quantity of snow to enable the hunters, by tracking the footsteps of the bear, to discover his retreats.

Aware of this advantage of being early in the mountains, I repaired to the Eaux Bonnes towards the end of April; but the rainy weather, which afterwards prevailed through the summer of 1835, precluding the possibility of hunting, I was forced, after waiting in vain for its cessation, to return to the low country. In May I returned again to the Eaux Bonnes.

*   *   *   *

One morning, after several days of unsuccessful hunting, which, in defiance of the rain and still more annoying mist which had almost constantly enshrouded the mountains, our eagerness to bring home an izard or bear had led us to undertake, the rattling of pebbles upon my bedroom window intimated that the hunters whom I had in my employ were underneath it. I was out of bed in an instant, and although so dark that I could scarcely distinguish the figures of my friends; still the first streaks of daylight shining above the mountains revealed the summits of the Pic de Gers, which since my return to Eaux Bonnes had been invisible. A few minutes sufficed for our preparations, and myself and two hunters were on our way up the mountain-side.

Hitherto we had gone out in parties, and the hunters acquainted with the passes by which the izards crossed from one summit to another, having posted one of us at each of them, made a sweep round the mountain, and endeavoured to drive the fleet little animals towards us. This is a savage style of hunting, and like all battues will not be relished by any one who entertains *liberal opinions* upon sylvan warfare. Upon this occasion, we were to endeavour to come upon the izards by stealth and cunning, the usual mode adopted by the Pyrenean hunters; or in other words, *stalk* them, as we do red deer in the Scottish Highlands.

The appearance of the morning was most favourable; not a speck of the mist was to be discovered, which had, with little interruption, hung upon the mountains for weeks, and whose presence had not only spoilt our sport, but upon more than one occasion had nearly proved fatal to some of our party [*].

[*] Upon one occasion in which a party of us were upon the flank of the Pic de Gers, the mist became so intense that it was impossible to see a few yards in advance of us. I and a friend, (who will not soon forget the circumstance,) had accompanied one of the hunters to a favourite izard pass high up the mountains, when the

Excepting in the very early part of the season, the mountains in the vicinity of the watering-places are so frequently *shot over*, that the izards desert them for the more solitary districts; and accordingly passing through the gorges of Balourd, and along the naked flanks of the Pic de Gers, we proceeded

mist increasing very much, it was deemed prudent to descend as rapidly as possible. This we endeavoured to accomplish, but among the turns and windings of the path, our guide mistook the route which we ought to have followed, and we found ourselves *brought up* at the foot of a perpendicular wall of rock, by a sheet of half ice, half snow, which but a few degrees removed in steepness from the rock above, sloped down the mountain-side, and right across the path which we were pursuing.

These patches of snow, especially when their outer coating has become hardened, and will not yield to the pressure of the foot, are most difficult to pass; and the many slips and falls which we had already had in crossing them where a roll in the snow was all the evil to be apprehended, made us dislike the appearance of the present wreath—so very much steeper than any which we had ventured to traverse, particularly as, should any of us chance to slip in the attempt, the mist prevented us having any idea of the character of the descent we should make. The wreath might terminate at the edge of a precipice, among a mass of fallen rocks, or in a snow-plain; but to us, who could only see a few yards down it, and could not explore its resting place except by descending it in a style which we would rather avoid, its nature was a matter of surmise.

We could not think of retracing our steps, we should have only bewildered ourselves among the rocks and snows which we had passed, and lost ourselves entirely. Accordingly I ventured upon towards the little valley of Sousouel, into whose lonely pastures the flocks and herds had not, as yet, found their way. Although so far advanced in the season, there was still a great quantity of snow remaining upon the mountains; and in the higher regions, if it had not been for the hot sun which

the wreath, my friend and the hunter watching my success. A staff of any kind would have been of great assistance; in lieu of it I was most unwillingly obliged to substitute my rifle, and to drive its barrel deep into the snow, to enable me to cling to my slippery path, which I crossed in safety. The breadth of the wreath could not exceed twenty paces; yet when I turned to look back, I could not distinguish the individuals who were upon the opposite side. My friend followed, adopting the same precautions which I had done, but with less success; for just as his figure became visible to me, he slipped, and going down the glassy surface like a shot, disappeared in an instant. I never shall forget the sensation which I experienced at the sight, although it was but of momentary duration; for a cry at no great distance below intimated that he was safe. Crawling down the edge of the wreath I reached the place where a softer portion of snow had slightly yielded to his weight, and ended his fearful course. He was still only half way across; but after resting for a minute or two to recover himself, he again started, and passed the wreath in safety. The hunter, after some deliberation, crossed where I had done, and after wandering about for some time in the mist, we gained the lower valleys without farther accident.

I had the curiosity, some days after this event, and when the weather had improved, to ascend the mountains for the purpose of searching for the spot where it had occurred, and discovering what beat upon our heads, we might have supposed that it was the month of January, from the wintry appearance of every thing around us. The snow was every where impressed with the traces of herds of izards, and we could frequently observe the deeply printed footmarks of the bear; in some places, where he had passed alone; in others, where a dam had been accompanied by her cubs. One of the latter tracks seemed so very fresh that we immediately set off at a brisk trot along it, and had followed it for several miles with apparent chance of success, when one of the hunters descried the objects of our pursuit at such a distance, traversing the steeps of the mountain above us, as completely to destroy our hopes of

would have been the result had my friend continued in his course down the snow wreath. After some little trouble, I found the place, and had it not been that the traces of our footsteps were quite fresh, I should have doubted the possibility of our having taken the route which we did. I mentioned that the wreath commenced at the foot of a perpendicular wall of rock; I now discovered that its resting place was a sloping terrace, which separated the foot of one precipice from the summit of another of fearful height; and that the spot where my friend had been enabled to stop himself, was within a very few yards of its edge, over which, but for the providential circumstance of one part of the snow being a little softer than another, he must have been dashed to pieces.

overtaking them. We watched them until they disappeared among the rocks, and then turned on our former course, regretting deeply that we had not crossed their path but one short half hour sooner. Shortly after, we met a shepherd who was returning from Sousouel, where he had been to examine the state of the pastures, and from him we learned that the flocks would be on their way to it on the following morning; and the more pleasing intelligence, that he had seen many izards in the valley.

Upon receiving this information regarding the appearance of the flocks on the morrow, the consequence of which would be the flight of the izards to the higher summits, we determined not to return to the Eaux Bonnes that evening, but passing the night under shelter of a pine, or in a shepherd's hut, if the winter storms had left any of them standing, to have another day's hunting. This being decided upon, one of the hunters was dispatched to the Eaux Chaudes (the nearest village) to procure an additional supply of provisions; for in our hurry in the morning, we had overlooked the probability of our being absent for a couple of days.

The want of this man might have greatly inconvenienced us; for in the event of our discovering a herd of izards in a situation where it was impossible to approach them, it would then be necessary to drive them, and one man is not always able to do this. But, as good fortune would have it, he was scarcely out of sight ere we encountered another hunter, whose presence (for he at once agreed to join in our expedition) far more than compensated to us for his absence. Our new comrade was no less a personage than Fonda, " le pere des chasseurs de la valleé d'Ossau;" and he well deserved the high title which had been conferred upon him. Every peasant who carries a gun aspires to the honour of being a chasseur; but it is only when the stranger who would enjoy the wild sports of the Pyreneés has the good fortune to meet with such a character as Fonda, that he can thoroughly appreciate the merits of a genuine hunter, and imbibe from him the necessary qualities of coolness, cunning, and hardihood, to render him successful.

Fonda is a native of Laruns, and was, when I met him, sixty-six years old, and had from boyhood been a hero of the wilds. He can boast of a descent more illustrious than many of the great ones of the earth ; for he can trace his descent in a direct line from heroes, who, like himself, had roamed in freedom among nature's grandest works, unfettered by the trammels of what is styled civilized society, but bound by the stronger ties resulting from simplicity and kindliness of heart. He was, when we met him, following the traces of the bears, and intended remaining out for several days in pursuit of them.

The appearance of the man who would thus singly search for, and encounter an animal of such strength and, when attacked, of such fierceness, as the Pyrenean bear, deserves description. Somewhat above the middle size, he has the high features, the dark eyes, the flowing hair, and muscular proportions, which characterize the inhabitants of the valley d'Ossau. Exposure to the storms of heaven, and the scanty fare with which he contents himself, have given him a look of even greater age than sixty-six ; and, to a casual observer, Fonda would appear a person ill-adapted for his profession. But, upon a little scrutiny, it will be discovered that it has neither been ill-health nor poverty which has withered the flesh upon his cheeks, and stamped the marks of age upon his countenance; the development of the muscles, the clear and fiery expression of the eyes, and the elasticity of the step, declare that Fonda is still a man of strength, if not of youth, and capable of enduring the exertions and fatigues of his pursuits.

In a pocket resembling the Highland *sporran*, he carried his balls, powder, and other articles for his gun; and, in a small knapsack, a spare shirt, a pair of spartillas, (to enable him to cross the slippery ledges of rock,) and the few pounds of bread which constituted his stock of provisions for some days. Previous to meeting him, I had been remarking to one of the hunters upon the extreme length of his gun-barrel; but that which Fonda carried astonished me still more. Excepting the articles which our gunsmiths are in the habit of putting up as signs at their shop-windows, I had never seen any thing resembling them. Above two centuries ago, there was a forge in the vicinity of Arudy, and there all the barrels of this description were made. They are smooth, and, although so very long, are exceedingly light, and have three or four *sights* along the barrel, not unlike those upon our rifles.

I asked Fonda how long it was since he had first possessed his gun; and he told me, that it had been the gun of his father, grandfather, and all his ancestors, since the period when it was manufactured. As a curiosity, it was a tempting one, and I offered him a sum for it which would have bought him a couple of new ones. It was a cruel offer to make a poor man, but it was rejected at once. The man and his gun were *in keeping*. Fonda, with a modern gun, would have appeared as ridiculous as the Gothic cathedral of Auch with its new Grecian columns; and it is not unlikely, that had he parted with his gun, and missed a few shots at first with the new one, that he would have thought it a punishment for having sold the heir-loom of his family; and, giving up his usual sports in disgust, died of a broken heart.

As soon as we entered the valley of Sousouel, we began to look eagerly for the izards which the shepherd told us he had seen. The track which the cattle and sheep have to pass, in order to get to the valley, winds along a ledge of the mountain considerably above it. On a sudden, the youngest of my companions laid his hand upon my shoulder, and drawing me towards the edge of the precipice along which he was walking, whispered to me to look over. Immediately below me, at the distance of six or seven hundred feet, was the little river of Sousouel, swollen into a torrent by the melting of the snows, and upon a rock by the edge of it, like a seal on the sea-shore, lay a solitary izard, basking in the sunshine.

We instantly drew back, to consider how we were to get within shot of him. This was soon decided upon; and, after one more stealthy glance over the precipice, to satisfy ourselves that we had not disturbed him, we left the spot. When started, the izard would at once make for the mountains, and Fonda pointed out the path which he would take. We had to cross it in our descent, and it had been proposed that one of us should remain near it, to intercept him, should he escape from the other two, who were to approach him under shelter of the rocks below; but Fonda, tossing a lichen into the air, declared that the wind was unfavourable for the pass, and that it would be useless to leave any one near it,—so extremely sensitive are the izards.

Our descent was extremely difficult, in many places very dangerous; but I was too eager upon the sport to waste a thought upon the subject. We were creeping down the steep in line; Pierre led the way, I followed, and Fonda came last; when, passing over a ledge of loose stones, one of them gave way under me, and I slipped and fell. I did not go far, but the stone rolled on, and I believed that all hopes of our shooting this izard were fled. Pierre saw the danger, and, regardless of the injury which he might sustain, deliberately laid his shoulder to the ground, to check the progress of the piece of rock. I dared not even whisper my thanks, nor ask him if he was hurt, so cautious was it necessary to be, and we kept our march in silence. We were still about a hundred and fifty yards from the bottom, when we found that we could descend no further, for, from the edge of the narrow shelf which we had reached, the precipice became too perpendicular to permit of our clinging to it.

I crawled along the ledge to a bend of the

rock from where we thought we might perceive the izard, and looking over, was upon the point of uttering an exclamation of disappointment, when I saw a block of stone which I supposed was that upon which I had first seen the izard, tenantless. I had mistaken the rock, for the izard was still there, dozing in fancied security. I had in my hand a double-barrelled gun, loaded with swan shot, and Pierre was carrying my rifle. Forgetting what I was about, I fired one shot at him as he lay, and a second as he started from the rock. Both the hunters fired about the same time, and the izard stood within a few paces of the rock from which he had bounded, perfectly unharmed, gazing around him, and wondering where the noise came from which had disturbed his slumbers. It was but for a moment; for he ascended the mountain directly towards where we were; he had not observed us, and took his accustomed path. I seized my rifle, and *slapped* at him, as he passed within a few yards of me, and —missed. I tell this story of my own defeat upon the first occasion in which I had a chance of being successful in izard hunting, as a warning to others who may be placed in a like situation, to behave more coolly than I did. Had I taken my rifle at first, I might have shot him as he lay upon the rock below; or, at all events, I could not have failed to have done so by reserving my double-barrelled gun until he passed me. Izards, when shot at, do not scamper off like other animals, but when they have proceeded a few hundred yards, stop, and look back upon those who have frightened them; thus it was with this fine old chamois, and he was almost within rifle-shot when he turned to gaze at us. I certainly could not distinguish the expression of his countenance, but I dare say it was that of scorn and derision.

Retracing our steps, we ascended the mountain, and, skirting along its side, entered one of the lateral valleys which branch off from that of Sousouel in the direction of Cauteretz. I now began to appreciate the merits of izard hunting, as pursued by the mountaineers, and to feel no wonder at their enthusiastic attachment to the sport. The side of the mountain, although very steep, was yet broken into a succession of small gorges, or water-courses, whose hollows (the favourite haunts of the izards) we had to examine most attentively, peering cautiously over the heights, ere we dared to descend into any of them. In this manner, many a mile, which, but for the constant excitement we were in, would otherwise have been felt fatiguing, was passed over, and we had not hitherto been able to get within shot of the watchful and suspicious little animals which we were in pursuit of, and whose heads we could frequently perceive disappearing over the crest of one ridge, as we mounted another.

It was now wearing late in the day, and I had almost begun to despair of retrieving the bad fortune of the morning, when Pierre descried an izard at rest among the rocks, a considerable distance in advance of us. Down we were on our faces in a moment; upon a further examination, it was discovered that there was a herd, and that the izard which had been first observed, was the sentinel on guard for the troop. To our sorrow, he had chosen a most admirable position for the purpose, for he had stationed himself upon a projecting ledge of rock, from which he could gaze above, below, and around him, far beyond gun-shot. We were now nearly at the head of the valley, and more than half-way up the mountain-side. The herd were in front of us, but we could not advance a step without putting them to flight, neither could we approach nearer to where they were, either by ascending or descending the mountain; so that, to me, they appeared to be completely out of danger from us. My companions were of a different opinion, and very soon decided upon the course which was to be taken.

The spot upon which we lay overlooked a pass, by which the izards ascended the mountains from their feeding-ground in the plains below; and here it was determined that I should remain, while the two hunters endeavoured to drive the herd along it. Pierre, making a circuit of several miles round the shoulder of the mountain which we had already passed, was then to cross by its summit to the upper end of the valley, and, descending by a deep ravine, place the herd between us; while Fonda, retrograding until he could reach the plain unobserved, was afterwards to approach to them as nearly as he could: so that, when Pierre should start them, he might be enabled to intercept them, should they attempt to cross the valley.

After they had left me, a slight haze which hung in the ravine cleared away, and I could distinctly see the herd, in groups of three or four together, feeding, or amusing themselves in the neighbourhood of their guard, in perfect security, confiding in his giving them timely notice of any danger which threatened them. In a short time, I could descry Fonda far below me, making towards the herd, sometimes by crouching on his hands and knees, sometimes by walking, as the inequalities of the surface permitted him, until he at length got near enough to them to effect his purpose.

It was three o'clock when we discovered this herd, and at half-past five Pierre had not as yet made his appearance. During this period I had been lying upon a patch of heath, well moistened by the melting of a snow-wreath which half encircled it; and, as may be supposed, was not only beginning to feel rather cold, but slight symptoms of a shivering fit were coming on, which would very soon have so unsteadied my hand, that I could not have taken an aim with any certainty; but a pull at my brandy-flask gave me temporary relief; and before its good effects had worn off, I could see Pierre a long way a-head of the troop. Down he came slowly and cautiously towards them. Then it was that I became afraid they should discover him too soon, and take to the mountains by a nearer path than that by which we hoped to make them pass; but a cat cannot hunt her prey with more dexterity than the hunters of the Pyreneés do the izards, and Pierre succeeded in this instance. When he thought that he had got near enough to the troop to effect his object, he uttered the shrill cry peculiar only to the mountaineers, and rushed forwards to where they were. As had been contemplated, the izards, upon hearing the noise made by Pierre above them, made off for the plain below. There, however, they could not go, for Fonda lay directly in their path, and he, anxious to drive them back, did not wait until the herd came so near him as to render it possible that they might pass by him when he showed himself, but started from his hiding-place and fired. The izards, confounded, halted for a moment, undecided where to go. It was still in their power to make for the mountains, by a path too distant for me to harm them, and to my vexation, they started for it. Pierre was, however, too knowing for them; he had, from the first, been aware of this chance, and the instant that he had roused the troop, he made direct for this path, in the hope of cutting off their retreat by it. But they were too fleet for him, and before he could reach it, they were "going the pace" along it. He had still another "string to his bow;"— another shout, and the discharge of his gun staggered them in their flight, and decided the day in our favour. They started off again, but the herd did not keep together; two of them took the path towards me, while the remainder held on their original course, and passing Pierre, were out of danger. Onwards the two came, bounding from crag to crag, and I had but time to decide upon the spot where I should fire at them, ere they had reached it. A low short whistle from me stopped them in their flight, my rifle-ball sped true, the foremost rolled down the steep, and its companion went off to join the troop upon the mountains.

On our return to the spot where we had proposed to pass the night, an incident occurred which sufficiently indicates the presence of mind evinced by the mountaineers, when placed in hazardous situations. The old chasseur was passing along a very steep face of rock, so steep that he had been obliged to exchange his leathern shoes for his spartillas, when an immense piece of rock, detached from the heights above, came bounding down the mountain side, directly towards him. I, who was higher up the mountain, and a considerable distance behind him, afraid that he might not observe the stone until it might be too late to get out of its way, shouted to give him warning, but I was too far off, and the falling mass was already within a hundred paces of him. Fortunately he could hear it bounding from the rocks in its descent, so that, aware what he had to expect, he prepared himself for the event. He remained stationary, gazing in the direction that the stone was descending; and when I thought that it must have crushed him, so very near had it approached to him, with the assistance of the long staff which he carried he sprang to one side, and the rock passed over the spot upon which he had stood.

In the early season, when the snows are melting, or after heavy rains, these falling rocks constitute one of the most serious dangers to which the hunters are exposed.

The herds of izards were now beginning to come down the mountains to feed; and, on our way to Sousouêl, we saw several very large herds. In crossing over a little knoll, we came in sight of a sheep-fold of the preceding year, in and around which the largest herd we had seen, induced, by the luxuriance of the herbage, had quartered themselves. They soon saw us, for we could not approach them undiscovered, and as they scampered up the hill, we counted sixty-two, old and young together.

Upon our arrival at the bottom of the valley, we found that our messenger for food had not returned, but that a shepherd's family, whose flock were coming over the mountains on the following day, had already constructed a covering of a few boards, under which to pass the night, and had lighted a huge pile of wood. We were not long in erecting a similar shed, for the boards and planks which had been in use the preceding summer, lay scattered around; and having lit another fire, we wanted nothing but the return of our caterer to feel perfectly satisfied with our situation.

The pastures of the little valley of Sousouêl are exceedingly rich; and during the period when the flocks and herds, and the many families who are engaged in making the cheese for which the valley d'Ossau is famous, are assembled in it, it is teeming with life; and the neighbouring woods, and the mountains, which rise from four to six thousand feet above the beautiful green sward of its surface, resound with the merry choruses and the shrill calls of the peasantry.

It was after ten o'clock, and we had begun to prepare our couch of the soft twigs of the box plant, and had made up our minds to go to bed supperless, despairing of the arrival of our messenger, when the wild mountain cry, which rose above the noise of the rushing stream, came most welcome to our ears. Pierre returned the cry, and, in a short time, guided by the sound, and the blaze of the fires, the absent hunter, and his well stored basket, made their appearance.

During the evening, Fonda related many of his adventures, and hair-breadth 'scapes in the mountains; but as these anecdotes properly belong to a chapter of a third volume, which may or may not, according to circumstances, find its way into the hands of the *devils*, and through them into those of the public, I shall conclude this chapter with the death-bed scene of this fine old hunter's father.

Like Fonda himself, he had been the unflinching and determined enemy of the beasts of the forest; and, for more than half a century, had been the most successful hunter of the district; and of bears alone, then far more numerous than they are now, he had killed no fewer than ninety-nine [*]. When upon his death-bed, and after he had received absolution of his sins, he observed to the priest, that he had still one heavy cause of uneasiness and regret upon his mind. "What can that be?" said the curé, "you have conducted yourself honourably in your transactions with your fellow men, and you die in the true

---

[*] The high rewards given by the communes, and the Prefet of the department, to the destroyer of a bear, and the great price for which the skin of the animal sells, have been the cause why so few are now to be met with in the Pyrenees.

faith, and pardoned for your sins, which have not been very heinous." "What you say is very true," answered the dying man, " but would that I had killed my hundredth bear!"

CHAPTER XXII.

Expedition to Eaux Chaudes in Winter—Pass of La Hourat—Its dangerous Character—Hotels of the Pyreneés in Winter—Scenery in the Valley of the Eaux Chaudes—Entrance to the Forest of Gabas—Village of Gabas—Mode of churning Butter—French Soldier—General Alava—Feelings of French Soldiery towards the Russians—Anecdote of a Bear Hunter—Forests of the Pyreneés—Magnificent Silver Firs—Unskilfulness of the Woodmen—Effects of the High Price of Iron in France—Troop of Spaniards—Le Cas de Broussète—Blind Spaniard—Cascade—The Frontier—Village of Sallient—Posada—Village Doctor—Family Scene—Political Dispute—Dance—Return to Bearn.

THE routes to the watering places of the Eaux Bonnes and the Eaux Chaudes are remarkably fine, and in their vicinity is scenery which for savage grandeur is almost equal to any in the Pyreneés. That around the Eaux Chaudes is of the most imposing character, and thither I shall now conduct the reader; not when its lodging-houses are filled with invalids, its wild paths crowded with convalescents, and the scorching rays of the summer sun beating overhead; but in the depth of winter, when the natives retreating to the lower and warmer situations, the village is almost deserted, and the falling avalanches alone disturb the stillness of the valley.

Few strangers think of penetrating into the mountains during winter, although they are then not less interesting than at other seasons of the year; perhaps even more so, for the snow and ice which render the low country altogether monotonous only adds to the character of the rugged and perpendicular sides of the mountains.

The apparent continuance of clear frosty weather, towards the end of December, was not to be resisted, and accordingly, accompanied by my friend and guide, Pierre, I set off for the mountains. When we arrived at Laruns, we found the snow very deep, and as it was late in the day, our acquaintances in the village strongly recommended us to rest there for the night, and not to proceed to the Eaux Chaudes as we intended. We were reminded of the probability of our encountering the Spanish Contrabandiers, some of whom are certainly not over particular as to their mode of living; and the likelihood that many parts of the road would be blocked up with the fallen snow. But it was bright moonlight, and we were not to be dissuaded from proceeding.

The ascent, to the magnificent Pass of La Hourat, the only entrance to the secluded valley of the Eaux Chaudes, was both tedious and fatiguing, from the quantity of snow through which we had to wade. The path which originally led to this watering place must have been scarcely better than an izard track, before the Princess Catherine, sister of Henry IV., opened up the present passage *.

* There is a small chapel, containing an image of the Virgin and Child, at the southern side of the pass, with an inscription commemorating the kindness of the Princess Catherine; and another, urging all those who enter the valley, to offer up a prayer to the Virgin, and prescribing the form of prayer to be used on the occasion. The following is a copy: "Chers voyageurs, nous voici entre les rochers fort escarpés, et l'affreux abime du ruisseau. Par ainsi ayons recours à la sainte Vierge. Qu'elle intervienne pour nous, que nous soyons garantis de tous dangers spirituels et corporels. Prière † *Pater* † *Ave*.

"Nous avons recours à votre assistance, sainte Mére de Dieu. Ne méprisez pas les prières que nous faisons dans nos besoins,

The narrow road has been cut—I might almost say *tunneled*—through the elbow of the mountain which encloses the valley, and carved along its almost perpendicular side for a great way, being, even now, little better than a shelf in the rock. The entrance to the Hourat from the southern side, was, as had been predicted to us, entirely blocked up with snow, forming a rampart many feet high in front of us. But drifted snow is, in frosty weather, in general so compact, that it may either be walked, or crawled over, and accordingly over the wreath we climbed upon our hands and knees. The road may, at this particular spot, be from twelve to fifteen feet in breadth, but the snow had obliterated all traces of it, filling it up, and forming a slope from the rock rising above it, to its further side, where the precipice dropped perpendicularly for several hundred feet down to the Gave below, whose waters thundered as they rushed through the narrow gorge, which in the lapse of ages, they had worn in the mountain-

mais délivrez nous en tous temps de tous périls et dangers. O sainte Vierge, remplie de gloire et de bénediction ! Nous, eglise de Laruns, ou prie pour.   F. S. Charlans."

side which obstructed their egress. Situated as the pass of the Hourat is, at the entrance to a long and narrow valley, into which several others open, there is almost always a severe blast of wind sweeping through the defile. I have frequently remained in it for hours in the sultry days of summer, enjoying the breeze, when there was not a breath of air stirring any where else. But most fortunately upon this occasion it was not of sufficient force to hurl us into the black abyss, as we wound our way slowly and cautiously, and as near to the rock as possible, uttering not a word, nor casting our eyes upon another spot than that where each hand, as it was clutched down, would, had it been possible, have willingly grasped a more secure tenure than that which the incrusted surface of a snow-wreath afforded.

The fearful slope was, however, passed in safety, and an hour's walking afterwards brought us to the Eaux Chaudes, where (as one of the hotel keepers resides in the village during the winter) I was soon seated at a comfortable fire, with a tolerable supper before me, and the prospect of a comfortable resting place for the night;

although, I must confess, that the hotels in the Pyreneés are not well adapted for winter quarters; considering that the best quality which they can possess is to be as cool and airy as possible. This in the summer heats is pleasant enough; but in winter, when one feels the curtains of his bed (if curtains there be) flapping in his face, and as a consequence, twitches of rheumatism in the morning; or when stepping out of bed, he finds his unprotected limbs refreshed by the snowy blasts direct from the mountains which, within a few hundred yards on either side, frown over him, he is apt to think that there must have been some negligence in their construction.

The fine weather continuing next morning, we resolved to cross the mountains into Spain, and sleeping at the Spanish village of Sallient, return the ensuing day. We left Eaux Chaudes very early, intending to breakfast at Gabas, the last village upon the French side of the mountains, and situated at the base of the Pic du Midi of Pau, the most remarkable mountain in the district. In the immediate vicinity of the watering-place the mountains are so very precipitous, and the sun, when it does shine forth in the winter, so powerful, that there is never a great deal of snow to be seen upon them, even when it is lying many feet deep in the valley; so that, although we miss the flocks and herds upon the steeps, still this valley has not the desolate appearance which others of the Pyreneés present in winter; and from the circumstance of its being one of the most frequented of the passes into Spain, there is always a considerable number of individuals engaged in the traffic between the two countries, travelling through it.

There are many splendid amphitheatric views in this valley; indeed from the Hourat to the Cas de Broussète it is a succession of almost unequalled scenery. One of the finest of these views is that which is beheld from the entrance to the forest of Gabas. There the road, but a few feet in breadth, sweeping round an elbow of the Som de Soube, skirts along its southern side; the river far beneath it is to be seen tumbling and tossing among the huge masses of fallen rock which impede its course, and laving the base of the Lacasol, which rises many thousand feet, clothed to a great height with the beech and silver fir, its bald and fantastically shaped crest conspicuous among the surrounding summits. In front is the Pic du Midi, its mighty fork, becoming still more imposing as it is approached, with its base covered with wood, stretching across the head of the valley, and leaving scarcely width sufficient for the river to pass between them, seems almost to touch the neighbouring mountain which completes the circle. The mountains in this district have a peculiarity which adds greatly to their beauty and interest. They are almost all detached from each other, forming distinct and separate mountains, a dozen of whose grey heads towering to the sky, may be observed from many points. The valleys which lie between them, are frequently little more than channels for the torrents; and their sides are generally, if not too precipitous, wooded; and even when so abrupt as not to admit of trees growing upon them, still the boxwood, plants of which are often of great size, finds a resting place on their steeps, and clothes their nakedness.

The village of Gabas consists of a few cottages, principally occupied by the soldiers of the Douaniers, who are stationed here to prevent the Spaniards or natives smuggling tobacco, and other contraband articles over the frontier; but who, nevertheless, contrive to elude their vigilance; for it is quite impossible to guard the paths over the mountains, many of which are perfectly unknown to the officers. Considerable quantities of Spanish wool is imported into France through this valley; and in return, the Spaniards take the shawls, handkerchiefs, and wines of Bearn.

Upon entering the little auberge where we were to breakfast, I found the owner, one of the finest looking men I ever beheld, engaged in making butter. The apparatus for churning was very simple in its character. The cream was put into a bag made of a small untanned lamb's skin, which had the wool taken off, and the aperture being tied up, the bag was shaken backwards and forwards until it was churned. The milk was then drained off, and perhaps half a pound or more of most excellent butter was rolled out of the skin. I breakfasted in company with an old soldier, and one of the most noted chasseurs of the district. The French soldiers are in general very jealous of the English, and are very seldom inclined to acknowledge that their opponents in arms on any one occasion ever gained a victory over them, which could not by them be most satisfactorily accounted for. I have met some French officers and soldiers who had wisdom enough to overcome this foolish prejudice, and candidly to review the events of the late war; but such individuals are not yet numerous, (although fast increasing in number, as a good understanding between the two nations is advancing,) and the Englishman when abroad must not be surprised to find even the victory of Waterloo a matter of controversy. I recollect a discussion taking place betwixt several of the French and English residents at Tours, as to whether victory would have declared in favour of Wellington at Waterloo, had the Prussians not made their appearance. It so happened that General Alava arrived in Tours while this discussion was at its height, and as he had been present at Waterloo, *en amateur*, and both parties considered him an impartial arbiter in the case, the disputed point was referred to him; when he gave it as his opinion, that even supposing that the Prussians had not come up before evening, the victory would have been declared for Wellington.

The old veteran whom I met at Gabas, bore willing testimony to the bravery of the British soldiers; and the encomiums which he bestowed upon the Duke of Wellington and the English army were very gratifying. " Ah!" said he, " the British and French have been brave enemies in time of war, and they ought now to be good friends in time of peace." He deprecated (as the French army universally do) the cruelty of leaving the Poles to the heartless mercy of their oppressors; and expressed his willingness, old as he was, to serve in a campaign against the Russians. This feeling towards Russia is very prevalent among the French soldiery, and I am very sure that they will gladly unite in any cause which has for its object the curbing of Northern ambition. The " Powers that be" in France, are well aware of this, and this knowledge is quite sufficient to restrain them from attempting to form too intimate an alliance with the Autocrat, however anxious they *might be* to do so.

The chasseur was my most particular friend; we had had many a long walk together over the neighbouring mountains, in pursuit of the izards or bears; and a better guide, or one who had more " hair-breadth 'scapes" to relate than Barras, was not to be found in the Pyreneés.

A rencontre which Barras had with a bear is worth narrating. It seemed that he had discovered a cavern, in which bruin had taken up his winter quarters, and from which he immediately determined to dislodge him. Single-handed he did not dare to attempt this, and accordingly he chose one of his most hardy companions to join him in the attack. The place which the bear had chosen for his retreat was an almost inaccessible cave on the side of the Pic du Midi, and among its darkest forests. When the two hunters arrived at the entrance of the cave, they consulted as to the best mode of rousing the animal, and getting him to leave it. Barras proposed that he should enter the cave, and wake him, while his companion stood guard without. This extraordinary mode of disturbing the bear's slumbers was adopted, and the sentry having sworn by the blessed Virgin to stand by his friend, the other prepared to enter the cave. For a considerable distance the cavity was large enough to permit of the daring hunter walking upright, but decreasing in height, he had to grope his way upon all fours. While proceeding in this manner, the bear, roused by the slight noise which the hunters had made at the entrance of his chamber, was heard approaching. To turn and run away was hopeless; the bear was too near to permit of this being attempted, so that to throw himself on his face, and take the chance of the animal's passing over him, was the only chance of escape. Barras did so, and the bear walked over him without even saluting him with a growl. His companion at the mouth of the cave did not get off so easily, for expecting that he would certainly have some warning of the approach of the animal, he was not altogether prepared for the encounter when he appeared, and ere he had time to lift his gun to his shoulder, he was folded in the deadly embrace of the giant brute. Within a few yards of the cave, the precipice was several hundred feet in depth, and in the struggle both bear and man rolled over it together. Barras, eager to aid his friend, followed the bear after it had passed over him, but reached the mouth of the cave just as the bear and his comrade were disappearing over the edge of the abyss. Horror-struck at the dreadful fate of his friend, and without the slightest hope of saving him, Barras rushed forward to descend the mountain-side, and rescue, if possible, his mangled body; when the first glance into the gorge below, revealed to him his friend dangling by his clothes among the branches of a thick shrub, which, growing out of a fissure in the precipice, had caught him in his fall, while the bear, less fortunate, had descended to the bottom. To release his friend from his precarious situation was no easy matter; but by the aid of the long sashes which the mountaineers almost always wear, he at last effected it, and drew him to the platform from which he had been so rudely hurled. The bear had lacerated him severely, but he was no sooner on his legs, than, expressing his confidence that the bear must have been killed by the fall, he proposed descending to the foot of the precipice to ascertain the result. This with much difficulty they effected, and to their great satisfaction, as well as profit, found among the rocks below the object of their search, in the last agonies of death. Sure of their prize, they returned to the Eaux Chaudes, the wounded man greatly exhausted by loss of blood; and Barras returning next morning to the field of battle, accompanied by a band of villagers, triumphantly carried off the spoil. The occasion upon which Barras related this adventure to me was a very appropriate one; we were then crouching together under a fallen pine of great size, watching a bear pass. I asked him how he relished bruin walking over him in the cave; he said he knew that his life depended on his remaining perfectly quiet; and he drew his large bony hand down my back, by way of indicating the feeling which the tread of the animal gave him.

Having breakfasted, and shaken hands with my friend Barras and the old soldier, Pierre and I proceeded on our journey across the mountains. Some of the Douaniers who had been out on duty by daybreak, informed us that the snow had drifted considerably during the night; and that in several places the narrow path which leads along the side of the Pic de Perilou to the Cas du Broussète was completely blocked up, and rendered impassable by the masses of snow which had fallen upon it from the rocks above; but after the affair of the preceding night, we thought little of their cautionary remarks.

A short distance from the auberge, we crossed the wooden bridge over the torrent which descends from the Pic du Midi*, and along whose brink there is also a path into Spain by the eastern side of that mountain, and one of the greatest beauty in the Pyreneés. That by which we travelled is upon the western side of the Pic. Forests of the most magnificent silver firs and beeches cling to the steep sides of the Perilou and the other mountains which we passed ere reaching the valley of Broussète, some of the trees (the silver firs) being of prodigious circumference and height. Many of these trees are cut down for the French navy, and considering the fine quality of the timber, and its size, it seems very extraordinary that the government do not evince a far greater degree of interest regarding the forests which produce them. There are officers of various grades from *Gardes Forestiers* to *Inspecteurs Generals* paid to take charge of the forests belonging to government, but each and all of them seem to know very little of the duties of their

---

* This beautiful and remarkable mountain is sometimes called the Pic du Midi of Pau, sometimes the Pic du Midi d'Ossau.

situations; and consequently, the greatest havoc and destruction are committed upon the woods, not only by the short-sighted and unthinking villagers, but by the workmen employed by government to cut them down. I have seen trees nearly twenty feet in circumference taken down by the hatchet, and so hacked and split in the operation as to be frequently left to rot where they are felled. Upon such occasions I have often wished that I could have shown the inexperienced natives and ignorant officials how neatly a couple of Scottish foresters with their cross cut saws would have taken down the trees. But the unskilfulness of the peasantry is not to be wondered at, neither is the simple nature of their tools a matter of astonishment. The selfish policy of the government is the cause of both. The price of iron is maintained so exorbitantly high, that none but the wealthier classes (and they but seldom) are in the practice of using it for any purpose where wood can be substituted. In the south of France a good useful spade is never seen, an iron rake very seldom; and their saws and other carpenter's tools are of a most inferior quality; indeed, in all their implements for agriculture and other purposes, the French are (as I once heard a liberal native of that country observe) a couple of hundred years behind us*.

Upon entering the valley of Broussète, in which we found a good quantity of snow, Pierre imagined that he descried a herd of izards at the upper end, and I immediately prepared my rifle. We watched their motions very anxiously, and almost buried ourselves in the snow to prevent their seeing us. On they came towards us, and just as I was congratulating myself upon my apparent good fortune, the herd of izards was transformed into a band of five and twenty or thirty Spaniards. From their marching in file among the inequalities of the surface, their *sombreras* had only been perceptible above the snow, so that the deception was very complete, and our astonishment at beholding the change, not little. But they

---

* The French people are becoming every day more and more awakened to the injurious character of the policy of their government upon the subject of the iron trade; and ere long will demand a repeal of the high duties on foreign iron. Until they attain this object, cheap iron cannot be procured in France; railroads can never be formed to advantage, even in the most populous districts; nor can the internal prosperity of the kingdom be advanced.

looked so exceedingly picturesque, almost each of them being clad in a different style of costume, and the whole of them such fine looking fellows, that, disappointed as I was, I did not *very* much regret their not being izards. They were on their way to Pau to purchase the manufactures of Bearn. Nearer the head of the valley, we met, returning from Spain, a troop of French peasants, accompanying a string of mules and horses loaded with sacks of wool. After passing the latter party, we found the track through the snow well beaten, and in many places opened up by cutting. Such troops in winter are always provided with axes and shovels, to clear away the ice and snow, which would otherwise obstruct their transit.

At the head of the valley is Le Cas de Broussète, the last habitation upon the French side of the frontier. The distance between the Spanish village of Sallient and Gabas being, even in summer, too far for one day's journey by those engaged in the commerce of the two countries, the French government have built the Cas de Broussète so as to divide the distance, and in winter obviate the danger of attempting such a passage across the mountains. The house is large and spacious, capable of accommodating several troops of merchants and their baggage; a hundred and fifty of whom are not unfrequently storm-staid in it for days or weeks together. Secluded among precipitous mountains covered with snow, or sheeted with ice, a more wild and lonely abode can scarce be conceived; or one whose solitude—but for the circumstance of there being a pathway practicable for horses leading by it over the frontier—runs less risk of being disturbed Three brothers have the care of this *Hospice*, who have constantly resided in it for many years, and have not during all that period ever quitted the valley, except when obliged to go to Gabas for provisions. Although they see little of the world, they see a great deal of *life*, and are frequently witnesses of scenes of boisterous mirth or ferocious quarrelling among the legal traffickers, the contrabandiers, and travellers who take refuge from the tempests in the Cas de Broussète.

The upper part of the valley is enclosed by ridges from the mountains which border it, up whose steeps the ascent is so rugged and dangerous that it seemed perfectly wonderful that the mules and horses could descend them loaded in the manner in which I have seen them. Half way up the ascent, we met an aged Spaniard carrying a heavy load of sheep skins upon his head. The poor old fellow, very insufficiently protected from the cold by his tattered clothes, was blind of an eye, and told us that he had sustained many severe bruises, from the falls which he had had among the crags. A draught from our flask was most thankfully accepted, and he proceeded on his toilsome march muttering blessings on us.

There is here in summer a very fine cascade. The river then rolls from a precipice of great height into the valley; but in winter it is calm and still, and when I passed it, a long perpendicular sheet of ice alone marked its course. After surmounting this ascent—the most difficult and fatiguing on the road—we entered another valley much smaller and less picturesque than the preceding, for in it there was not a vestige of wood, and the mountains which enclose it are inferior in height and character.

An hour's walk brought us to the frontier. The boundary is, as usual, marked by the watercourses; where the water runs towards Spain, that is Spanish ground; where towards France, it is French. Independent of this circumstance, nature seems to have otherwise pointed this place out as the limits of the two countries. Upon the immediate frontier, the aspect of the kingdoms is altogether different. In the French territory appear the blue rocky mountains, hanging with wood, and interspersed with fine pastures even among their highest altitudes. In the Spanish, the sudden alteration of the strata renders the valley and surrounding mountains most sterile and desolate; their rocks look as if they had been on fire, and their ashes scattered around. A few spots of herbage in this waste, only make its barrenness more marked. In summer, however, the dreary appearance of this valley must be somewhat enlivened by the beautiful flowers of the rhododendron, plants of which I observed peeping from beneath each rock where a particle of soil could be obtained.

The village of Sallient is about five hours' walk from the frontier, so that by the time we reached it, it was almost dark. It is situated upon an eminence at the junction of several valleys, and from the circumstance of the backs of the houses being placed towards the mountains, and their regularity in height*, and want of windows, the village, or rather town, for it is of considerable extent, has much the appearance of a fortification, and could easily be rendered such in time of war.

In the preceding summer, Pierre had accompanied the lady of the Belgian Ambassador across the mountains to the baths of Pentacousse by this path, upon which occasion they had slept at Sallient; he was, therefore, acquainted with the localities of the place; so that after threading our way for some time through a labyrinth of dirty lanes, we found the posada where we were to spend the night. A small wicket in a door which filled a large archway admitted us into the lower part of the building, which, as usual, was, apportioned to the bestial portion of the establishment, the winter's fuel, casks of wine or *aqua ardente*, and other stores. Upon hallooing for some of the inmates to descend, and conduct us through the windings of the place, a little urchin came down a trap-stair at the further end bearing in his hand a piece of blazing pine. By the

---

* In the Spanish villages the houses are almost universally two stories in height.

light of this brand we were enabled to steer clear of the heels of the mules, unsaluted even by a stray kick, which few strangers who pass through the under hall of a Spanish posada are not threatened with, and reached the principal room of the house, which served the joint purposes of kitchen and salle-à-manger. Here we found crouching round a wretchedly bad fire, the señora of the house, her eldest daughter, a girl of nineteen, and half a score of boys and girls under that age. It is very seldom that any strangers, above the rank of those engaged in the traffic across the frontiers are seen in this village, so that our arrival created considerable bustle among the members of the family. A fresh supply of fuel was brought from the stores below and heaped upon the hearth, a few additional pieces of lighted pine stuck in the sides of the chimney, illuminated the apartment, and the hostess prepared our supper.

Meanwhile Pierre and I having pulled off our wet clothes, seated ourselves on the bench, which, like those of our lowland cottages some years ago, almost encircled the fire place. There we had not long established ourselves, ere the landlord, (who was also the Maire of the village,) accompanied by several other individuals, entered the room, muffled up to the throat in their dark mantles. The costume of the Arragonese peasantry in winter is by no means pleasing. They are then seldom without their dark cloaks, underneath which they wear jackets and small-clothes of the same sombre hue, unornamented, as is generally the case even among the poorest of the peasantry of other districts. Beneath their huge sombreras, which they seldom lay aside but when they sleep, they wear a coloured Bearnais handkerchief twisted round their heads. Curiously wrought blue or white worsted stockings and sandals complete the dress of the men. That of the women is generally of blue woollen cloth made tight to the figure, and beneath the waist exceedingly full. Their head dress is either composed of a white or coloured cotton handkerchief, but never so tastefully arranged as those of their Bearnais neighbours.

The host, after the usual salutations, immediately inquired if I knew how the war was going on. I pleaded total ignorance on the subject, aware that the less I talked upon the subject on the Spanish side of the frontier, to individuals whose politics I had had no means of ascertaining, the less chance there was of my creating suspicions as to my motives for entering the country. Apparently satisfied that I knew little of the actual state of the war, he left me to join his companions, who in the further end of the apartment were loudly debating upon a matter seemingly of much interest to them, and relating to which one of them held in his hand a long roll of papers. Somewhat curious to ascertain the cause of their discussion, I made Pierre ask the señora if she was acquainted with the reason of it, when she told us that it was "settling night" with the doctor of the village, and that the papers contained a list of the inhabitants who were indebted to him. The mode of paying the Esculapius of the place, was by each family compounding for his attendance for a certain yearly sum. Ten francs for each house would, in so large a village as Sallient yield a very tolerable income to the doctor, and ought scarcely to have been considered an exorbitant sum by the householders to pay for having their bodily health taken care of. But they grumbled sadly at the tax, especially those who had not required any attendance; while those who had been ill, complained of the additional expense of the medicines. The landlord, in particular, was very wroth at being obliged to pay as much as eight francs for the potions which his family had swallowed during the preceding year, and asked me if I did not consider the sum of eighteen francs a year, an immense sum to pay the doctor for his advice and medicines. Fifteen shillings a year might be a large sum to the inhabitants of a poor Spanish village, but there seemed to be no mode of getting rid of the tax, grumble as they might at its infliction, as they presently, although very reluctantly, marched off to pay it, and left us to pick our supper from a few *spare* ribs of mutton, which the señora had grilled for us among the embers of the fire.

Spanish women are proverbial for the beauty of their eyes, and those of this family were certainly by no means calculated to create dissent from the general impression, and none to which the term "speaking eyes" could more truly be applied. In those of the mother (a woman of forty years of age) intrigue was written in most legible characters, while in those of the daughter, it seemed almost as intelligible. In the course of the evening, I was exceedingly amused by the care which the ladies took to prevent the host witnessing the slightest familiarity between them and any of the men who came into the posada. The daughter, and more frequently the mother, would be seated beside some handsome mule-driver or smuggler, whose arm (seeing that there was no back to the benches on which they sat) was very naturally entwined round their waists. Mine host did not, however, seem to relish this substitute for a chair-back, and consequently the slightest suspicion of his entrance sufficed to throw the fireside circle into commotion; away flew the females to wash the plates and dishes, and the men seemed engaged in fastening their spartillas. On one occasion the host entered so abruptly that, had it not been for the instantaneous presence of mind of the daughter, I should have been witness to a scene of a most unpleasant character. The mother, supported in the manner I have mentioned, had not time to start from her seat, but the moment her husband entered, his daughter (who happened to be then crossing the apartment) dropped a plate as if accidentally. His attention was drawn to it, and the situation of his partner was unobserved. Picking up a fragment of the plate, and holding it as if he intended throwing it at the girl, he cursed her for her carelessness. She, however, saved her mother's life by the act, for I am confident that had there been no plate broken on the occasion, that the knife would have been called into requisition, and one or both of the delinquents been killed, for what, in any of our country inns, the landlord would have beheld with comparative indifference. No class of Spaniards are more *ready* with their knives than the Arragon, and none who can use it more effectually. Their knife is rather longer than that of the peasantry of other districts, and though a clasp knife, is a weapon of the most deadly nature. The mode in which they use it is by grasping the case, with their thumb resting upon the under part of the inside of the blade, which is blunt, and then drawing down their arm to its full length, they strike upwards invariably, driving the blade into their antagonist's body until their thumb prevents its further entrance. Such a wound is almost always a fatal one, and the traveller in Spain must be cautious how he renders himself liable to such attacks from his intimacy with pretty faces and intriguing eyes.

In the course of the evening, many of the villagers had assembled in an adjoining room, to sip their wine, and talk over the politics of the day. There were among them supporters of both the great parties contending for the sovereignty of the country; each of them anxious for the success of the cause he had espoused. As usual in such discussions, the longer that the argument lasted, the more warm became the debate, until the voices of the speakers were so elevated, that the señora, accustomed as she no doubt was to such scenes, was alarmed for the consequences. There seemed every probability of the *argumentum ad hominem* being put in requisition by the contending factions, when one of the party, more wise than the rest, commenced in a fine and powerful voice one of their national songs. The effect was electrical, the disputation instantly ceased, and one and all of them joined in the chorus. After several songs had been sung, and the harmony of the party completely restored, the landlord came and asked me to join them. I accepted the invitation, and was most cordially welcomed. In honour of the stranger a dance was proposed, and the wives and daughters of the individuals present were soon assembled together. Here, as in Andorre, and in other Spanish villages, the instruments were the guitar and triangle. Both men and women danced uncommonly well, and displayed as much spirit as I ever beheld in a Highland reel; several hours' continued dancing scarcely seemed to abate their ardour. The younger girls danced beautifully, and it was wonderful the exertion which they endured; for the gentlemen being far more numerous than the ladies, each man, when he thought his friend had exhibited long enough, elbowing him out, took his place, and thus their partners had no respite.

At last I "stole away" to my old corner at the kitchen fire, and soon after, the party broke up. The chamber in which I was to sleep contained a couple of beds, which Pierre told me, upon the last occasion that he visited the posada, were occupied by the Belgian Ambassadress and her maid, while he slept on the floor of the room in the honourable capacity of guard to her Excellency. The half dozen gentlemen who were of the party, were obliged to roll themselves in their cloaks, and sleep on the floor of the kitchen, a situation not at all relished by the delicate Parisiens. Had it been summer, I should have much preferred dozing on a bench or table, to trusting myself between the sheets of a posada bed; but the winter's cold had destroyed certain bedfellows very common in France and Spain, and the wearied traveller, at that season of the year, could feel satisfied that his place of repose would not be converted into one of torture.

While engaged in heaping as many cloaks upon our beds as we could find, the door of our room was opened, and the young lady of the house, carrying a pine torch, entered, followed by a young Spaniard, (her favourite I believe,) who was very tipsy. She conducted him by a trap-stair which mounted from our room to his bed in the attic above, and after some little delay, occasioned, I presume, by her showing him the direction in which it stood, she returned, bringing the light with her. In the poorer Spanish houses there are neither candles nor lamps, and the mode of lighting the apartments is by means of pieces of blazing pine placed upon a flat piece of iron suspended from the wall; and these pines of the country being full of resin, a few slips are sufficient to light a large room.

Next morning, I found the whole of the party of the preceding night assembled in the posada, to request me to remain a day or two longer in their village. But this I could not have done, even had I been inclined, as I had forgotten to bring a passport with me; so that, having breakfasted, and taken leave of the villagers of Sallient, we returned across the mountains to Bearn.

APPENDIX.

SKETCH, DESCRIPTIVE OF THE FORMATION, APPEARANCE, AND CHARACTER OF THE PYRENEES.

THE Pyreneés are that chain of mountains which divide the Spanish peninsula from France, and which extend from the *Cap de Cervere,* to the south-east of *Colliouvre,* or, rather, from the *Cap de Creus,* near *Rosas,* upon the shores of the Mediterranean, to the point of *Figuier,* near *Fontarabia,* on the Bay of Biscay.

It is almost generally supposed, that the Pyreneés are an isolated chain of mountains, from the circumstance that their extremities drop into the sea; but a glance at the maps of France or Spain will be sufficient to determine that the Pyreneés form but a part of the system of the mountains of the two countries. In short, the Pyreneés appear to be attached, on the east, to the great chain of the Alps, by the *Montagne Noire*, and the *Cévennes;* and to the west, long before they dip into the ocean, at the point of *Figuier*, they stretch away to Cape *Ortegal*, in *Galicia;* so that their apparent termination at the point of *Figuier*, is merely that of a lateral branch, which detaches itself from the principal chain at the head of the valley of the *Bastan*. In like manner, their junction with the *Montagne Noire*, and the *Cévennes*, is effected by means of another lateral chain, which branches off to the east of the valley of the *Teta*, in the French *Cerdagne*.

Excepting in a few instances, the boundaries of the two countries are fixed by the course of the waters from the summits of the central ridge; the land to the north of the division of the streams belonging to France, and that on the south appertaining to Spain.

The French departments situated upon the frontier with Spain, are, beginning on the east, those of the *Pyreneés Orientales*, the *Arriège*, the *Haute Garonne*, the *Hautes Pyreneés*, and the *Basses Pyreneés*. The department of the *Aude*, although at some distance from the central chain, contains, nevertheless, mountains which belong to the Pyreneés; and these are the branches generally known as the mountains of the *Corbières*, a part of the connecting link between the French and Swiss mountains. The ancient provinces of France comprised in these departments, are the *Vallspir*,

Roussillon, the *Conflens*, the *Cerdagne*, the *Capsir*, the *Donnezan*, the *Pays de Sault*, a part of *Languedoc*, the county of *Foix*, the *Couzerans*, *Comminges*, the *Quatre valleés*, *Bigorre*, *Béarn*, the *Pays de Soule*, *Basse Navarre*, and the *Pays de Labourd*.

The Spanish provinces adjoining the Pyreneés are *Catalonia*, *Arragon*, *Haute Navarre*, and *Biscay*.

The length of the Pyreneés, from east to west, is about two hundred miles; and their breadth very varied. It is greater in the centre than towards the extremities of the chain, but may throughout be averaged at sixty miles.

The Pyreneés are seen from a great distance, from whichever side they are regarded. One of the most favourable points from which to enjoy a view of the greater part of this magnificent chain, is from the hills called *Pech David*, to the south of Toulouse. There the spectator is placed nearly in front of the centre of the range, sufficiently distant to admit of a vast horizon; and yet near enough to distinguish their most remarkable features. From the *Pech David* the Pyreneés may be seen for more than a hundred and fifty miles, from the *Canigou*, in *Roussillon*, to the great summits at the head of the valley *d' Ossau*, in the *Basses Pyreneés*.

The appearance which they present is extremely imposing; they appear to form one single mountain, increasing in height towards the east, but broken into summits of various forms and characters. But the aspect of the mountains is not always the same, depending entirely on the state of the atmosphere, the hour of the day, and the season. There are many days, however, throughout the year, when the purity of the air is sufficiently perfect to admit of all the summits being seen which are visible from Toulouse. It is in the beginning of Spring, or towards the end of Autumn, that this magnificent sight is to be most distinctly seen, and the hours most favourable for beholding it, are those immediately after sunrise, and before sunset; the sky is then more free from vapour, the outline of the mountains is better defined, and their shades more deeply marked. During the prevalence of the west and north winds, the Pyreneés are, most frequently, shrouded in mists, particularly towards their eastern extremities.

The direction of the Pyreneés is, as has been already noticed, from east-south-east to west-north-west; nevertheless, the range does not pursue a direct line, but is on the contrary composed of two parts, or two lines, which are indeed parallel in their course, but are not the continuation of each other. Thus, if we divide the chain into two parts towards the centre, we should find that the half situated upon the west was considerably further south than that upon the east; and that two lines, one drawn from the eastern, and the other from the western extremity of the range, would throughout their course, be at least thirty miles distant from each other. The *Garonne*, the most beautiful river of the Pyreneés, has its source among the mountains at the junction of the two chains. The eastern chain is terminated in the valley of the Garonne, by the mountain called *Tentenade*; but the point at which the mountains, linking the two chains together, separate from the eastern one, is at the *Tuc* du Mauberme*; and the *Port d'Espot* the point at which they unite with the western.

The Pyreneés have, to the south and to the north, many lateral branches, which gradually decrease in height as they recede from the central range, until they are lost in the plains more or less distant from the foot of the mountains. There are, however, some exceptions to this general disposition. A few of these lateral ranges maintain a great altitude throughout their whole length and are terminated by mountains of considerable height; others, on the contrary, terminate ere they have left the mountains, generally at the junction of two valleys. Besides these branches, which, like buttresses for the support of the central ridge, stretch off laterally on both sides of it, there are also a considerable number of minor chains, which take a direction similar to the great one. The most remarkable of these minor chains are to

* The word *Tuc* has, in the patois of the *Couzerans*, the district in which that mountain is situated, the same signification as *Pic*.

be found in the departments of the *Arriège* and the *Basses Pyreneés*. The point at which two of these branches commence is generally marked by the increased height of the great ridge, and the source of opposite valleys by the diminution. These depressions at the heads of the valleys constitute the natural passages by means of which the peasantry are enabled to pass from one to another. In the Alps, and towards the extremities of the Pyreneés, they are called *Cols;* but, in the centre of the chain, they are known by the name of *Ports*. The first of these terms is used in the departments of the *Pyreneés Orientales*, and the *Basses Pyreneés**; and the second in those of the *Arriège*, the *Haute Garonne*, and the *Hautes Pyreneés*.

Ramond, and other celebrated naturalists, are of opinion, that the southern slopes of the Pyreneés, are the most steep and rapid; and what I have seen of the Spanish sides of the mountains leads me to confirm their assertions. There the ascents are invariably more steep and rugged, and, consequently, more difficult and

---

* In *Basse Navarre*, which forms a part of this department, the *Cols* are called *Lepoa*, a word which in the Basque language, has precisely the same signification as *Col*, which signifies literally the *neck* (le cou) of the mountain.

The terms *Partillon, Cot, Hourque, Hourquette, Fourque, Fourquette, Porte, Breche*, &c., have all the same signification, and are used indiscriminately with those of *Col* and *Port*.

fatiguing. Almost the whole of the French valleys either ascend gradually to the central ridge, or by a succession of basins. On the Spanish frontier this is seldom the case; and in the vicinity of the highest mountains,—of Mont Perdu, for instance,—we find the Spanish summits decrease in altitude very suddenly, dwindling almost into insignificance at its base; while, on the French, or northern side of that great mountain, there are very many summits but little inferior in height to its own.

I have already observed that the Pyreneés, as they approach the coasts, decrease in height very rapidly. This depression of the mountains commences much sooner at one extremity than at the other. Thus, there is no considerable summit within twenty-two or twenty-three leagues of the Bay of Biscay; while the Canigou is within less than fifteen of the Mediterranean.

The Pyreneés contain a great number of valleys. All the great valleys are transversal. They begin at a *Col* in the ridge of the central chain; and, taking their course directly to the north or south, they form nearly a right angle with it.

The valleys of the greatest length are those situated towards the centre of the range. These are, the valleys of the *Garonne*, and the *Lavedan*, the latter watered by the *Gave of Pau*, which unites with the *Adour*, a few miles above *Bayonne:* the length of the first is about fifteen leagues; the second about thirteen. The longitudinal valleys, or those whose direction is parallel with the centre range, are in general of very small extent; most frequently mere ravines, or gorges. The most considerable of the number is that of *Massat,* or *Soulan,* and that of the *Bastan**; in which are situated the famous baths of *Barèges.* Their length is six or seven leagues.

The valleys which terminate in the plains at the northern base of the Pyreneés are sometimes broad and open at their entrance, sometimes exceedingly confined. Among those of the first class are the valleys of the *Tech,* of the *Teta,* of the *Arriège,* of the *Sallat,* of the *Lavedan,* of *Ossau,* and many others. The valley of the *Garonne,* and those of *Aure,* of *Aspe,* of *Baigorry,* &c., are, on the other hand, extremely narrow at their entrances, as are, almost without exception, both the transversal and parallel valleys of these mountains.

There are very few of the valleys of the Pyreneés, which, throughout their course, do not present a succession of basins. These basins are formed by the mountains which border the valley receding from the banks of the river, and leaving a circular hollow, where there is so

---

* There are two valleys of this name in the Pyreneés, one appertaining to France, the other to Spain; but they are situated at such a distance from each other, that they are seldom, or never, confounded with each other.

slight a declivity, that the stream undulates slowly through its whole extent, assuming a character in accordance with the quietness of the scenery around it: until at the extremity of the basin, where the mountains again close in upon it, and confine it in its course, it resumes its original character, and dashes through their gorges, and over their precipices. These basins are, in general, considerably elevated above each other, and are joined together by narrow and deep ravines, rapidly inclined plains, or by a slope of rock so very perpendicular, that the river dashing over, forms a cataract from the basin above to that beneath. They are more frequent in the upper part of the valleys, and are there better defined and more remarkable in appearance than in the inferior, where they are much less perfect; although, at the same time, they seem, from the marks of destruction which they bear, to have, in other times, been as complete as those in higher situations, where, hitherto, there has never been such accumulations of the waters, as to have destroyed their comparatively level surface, by working through, or destroying the precipice or slope, over which their rivers rush in unbridled turbulence. The quantity of alluvial matter which they contain, is also conclusive evidence that these inferior basins were at one period as perfect as the others.

The hollows, or basins, in the upper districts of the valleys, frequently contain lakes, whose extent is proportionate to the dimensions of the basin. These lakes are very common in the Pyreneés, and are to be found in almost all of the valleys on their northern side. On the Spanish side, they are seldom to be met with; a fact that may almost be thought sufficient to establish as correct the opinion that the southern sides of the Pyreneés are far more steep and rapid than the northern.

When these lakes, which are never of great extent, are found at such heights as to be surrounded by glaciers and perpetual snows, they are generally covered with ice throughout the year. Thus the lakes of the *Port d'Oo*, and the *Portillon d'Oo*, are always frozen; and the lake of *Mont Perdu*, and those of *Estom-Soubiran* in the valley of Cauteretz, are covered with ice until the end of August. The basins also, which are now-a-days merely watered by the river which flows through their centre, bear incontestible evidence of the existence of ancient lakes, of which they were the beds. Their soil so often marshy or full of peat, their rocky sides far above their surface, bearing marks of the ravages of the waters; and the manner in which the torrent breaks away from these basins by a deep and narrow gorge, are the proofs that they have in other times been lakes hemmed in upon all sides; and that they are only now drained by means of the breach which their superfluous waters have forced in the bed of rock which inclosed them.

At the junction of various valleys and gorges, there is

APPENDIX. 263

always one of these basins; and it is a general rule in the Pyreneés, that the extent of the basin is in proportion to the number and width of the lateral valleys, ravines, and gorges which open into it*; and that when a valley suddenly alters its direction, the elbow thus formed is invariably followed by one of them.

The largest of these basins do not exceed eight miles in length, by three or four in breadth. Such are the magnificent basin of *Argélèz*, in the valley of the Lavedan, of *Bagneres*, in the valley of Luchon, and of *Bedous*, in the vallée d'Aspe. It is generally in the inferior part of a valley that we find the basins of the greatest extent, because there the greatest number of tributaries unite with them.

The mountains which skirt a valley very seldom ascend unbroken to their summits, but, in general, attain their full height by many slopes, more or less rapidly inclined. At the base of these successive slopes are little plains, and the number of these slopes and plains depend altogether upon the altitude of the mountains, and the nature of the rocks which compose them. We almost constantly find that the stratum which lies along one side of a valley, corresponds with that upon the

---

* It is from an observation of this nature that *M. Palassou* draws his strongest arguments against the opinion of those geologists who attribute the formation of the valleys to the currents of the ocean.

other; and that if there is a plain upon the heights on one side, there is a corresponding plain upon the other. This circumstance would seem to prove, that the soil of the valley has, at some period or other, been of the same height with the plains upon each side of it, and that the waters have, in the lapse of ages, worn it down.

This arrangement of the slopes is most apparent in the upper districts of the valleys, because the mountains which are situated in the lower are, comparatively speaking, so much inferior in height, that the terraces or plains which we find at greater elevations, have disappeared, and there is but one continued slope from their base to their summit.

These observations regarding the plains or table lands to be found among the Pyreneés, and the circumstance of their generally corresponding with others situated on opposite sides of the valley upon which they are found, is most decidedly characterized in the valley of *Héas*, which opens into that of the *Lavedan*, near the village of Gèdre. The valley of *Héas* is found to contain two of these plains, which, at a great height above the stream which runs through it, extend from one extremity of it to the other. The plain which we observe upon the left hand is that of the *Coumelie*, upon the mountain of the same name; and upon the opposite side, that of the *Camplong*, of the same height as the preceding one. The rock which composes the soil of the valley, and of the mountains below these plains, is granitic; the whole of the mountains above them to their summits are, on the other hand, formed of shiste or limestone; thus evidently from this coincidence it would seem that these plains were at one period the *bottom* of the valley, until the torrents wore out the great gulf between them *.

There is little appearance of order in the formation of the valleys at those points where two or more of them unite; we there find the various strata of which the Pyreneés are composed confused together, the primary and the secondary formations united; and not unfrequently, as in the case of *Mont Perdu* and others, we

---

* These facts, however numerous, cannot establish the doctrine of many geologists, that all valleys have been formed by the receding of the seas, or the destructive influence of the rivers; as there exist many incontestible proofs of their having been formed by depression, or by some convulsion of nature heaving up the mountains which border them. One remarkable instance of this nature, occurs to me at this moment. It is the valley of the Devon in Clackmannanshire. There we have abundant proof that a convulsion of nature has created it. We there find the strata upon both sides of the valley, not lying in a horizontal direction, as in those valleys supposed to have been formed by the waters, but dipping, like an inverted arch, through the hollow of the valley, and, rising on both sides of it, appearing in the form of a pack of cards resting against an inclined plane—the inclined plane being the hills which inclose it. Depression or convulsion could alone have formed such a valley.

also find the once prevailing opinion of geologists, that the highest mountains of the European continent were those of primitive rock, confuted, and a mountain of secondary formation rearing its head above the primitive ones around it.

The source of many of the Pyrenean valleys is a hollow, or, as it is styled in the Pyreneés, an *Oule**, surrounded by walls of perpendicular rock, excepting towards the point where the waters collected in it have worn for themselves a passage, through which they leave it. The walls which surround these basins or *Oules*, are most frequently called *Cirques*, and sometimes, from the successive slopes and perpendicular masses of rock which surmount them, *Amphitheatres*.

The most beautiful of these *Circles* is that of *Gavarnie*, at the source of the valley of the Lavedan. That Circle is not, perhaps, the most extensive in the Pyreneés, but the walls which surround it are the highest and most perfect. In all the other great circles, the walls are more or less unequal in their height, and more or less perpendicular. The Circle of *Troumouse* at the source of the valley of Héas, is larger than that of *Gavarnie*, but the rocks which inclose it are far less remarkable in appearance. The Circle at the source of the valley of *Estaubé*

---

* *Oule*, or *Houle*, or *Ouil*, is a word in patois signifying a *large pot* or *kettle* (*marmite*).

is still less perfect in its formation. There are also many other of these Circles in the Pyreneés less worthy of notice than those which I have mentioned; among them are those at the source of the valleys of *Ossonne*, and *Treimbareil*, and all those which open into the valley of *Barèges;* and those in the valley of *Betmalle*, at the foot of the *Roque de Balam*, and in that of *Uret*, both of which valleys are tributaries of the valley of *Castillon*.

M. Charpentier, the latest geological writer upon the Pyreneés, makes the following observations upon the formation of their valleys. " Lorsqu' on considère la constitution physique des vallées, et les divers phénoménes qu' elles présentent, on reconnaît facilement que leur excavation ne peut pas être le résultat ni de courants de mer, ni d'affaissements ou de soulèvements des montagnes, mais celui d'une chute ou descent constante des eaux. Il est plus que vraisemblable que les Pyreneés, lorsqu' elles sortirent de la mer où elles sont nées, n'ont formé qu' une seule longue montagne en forme de dos d'âne ; que les deux pentes n'étaient point unies, mais presentaient des creux, des enfoncements et d'autres inégalités ; que les eaux qui remplissaient ces creux ou bassins ont épanché leur trop plein par la voie la plus convenable aux lois de la pesanteur, et du coté où elles éprouvaient la moindre résistance ; et qu' enfin, en se versant des bassins supérieurs dans les bassins inferieurs, elles ont du insensiblement excaver et creuser les rochers qui séparaient un bassin de l'autre, agrandir ces mêmes bassins, élargir et approfondir les canaux, pour m'exprimer ainsi, par lesquels elles s' écoulaient d'un réservoir à l' autre, et former de cette manière peu a peu de vastes conduits, auxquels ou a donné le nom de *vallées*."

The truth or incorrectness of this hypothesis of Charpentier's, I shall leave more learned geologists than myself to support or refute.

The principal valleys which have their source on the northern side of the central ridge of the Pyreneés are, beginning upon the east,

The valley of the *Tech*. This valley opens upon the plains of Roussillon, near the town of *Boulou*, and its river runs into the Mediterranean a short distance from Elne.

The valley of the *Teta*. This valley also opens upon the plains of Roussillon; and its river flowing near Perpignan, falls also into the Mediterranean.

The valley of the *Aude*. The river of the *Aude* leaves the mountains in the vicinity of *Limoux*, and flowing near *Carcassonne* empties itself into the Mediterranean about six leagues from Narbonne.

The valley of the *Arriege*. This beautiful valley terminates in the plains of Languedoc, between *Foix* and *Pamiers*, and its river flows into the *Garonne*, near the village of *Portet*, a league above Toulouse.

The valley of *Vicdessos*. This valley, famous for its

iron mines and forges, is a tributary of the preceding, and joins it near the town of *Tarascon*.

The valleys of *Aulus* and *Ercé*.

The valley of *Ustou*. These three valleys join the great valley of the *Sallat;* the two first near the village of *Oust*, and the last near the little hamlet called *Lepont-de-la-Taule*.

The valley of the *Sallat*. This valley opens into the plain near *Saliex*, and its river, the *Sallat*, unites with the *Garonne* a little below *St. Martory*.

The valley of *Castillon*, or the *Castillonaise*. Its river, the *Lers*, joins the Sallat near *Saint Girons*. The upper part of this valley is generally called the valley of *Biros*.

The valley of *Ger*, or *Aspect*. The torrent of this little valley falls into the Garonne near the village of *Montespan*, a couple of leagues from *St. Gaudens*.

The valley of the *Garonne*. This valley, the longest of the Pyrenees, terminates in the plains of *Comminges*, between *Saint Bertrand*, and *Montrejeau*. From its source in the mountains of Spain to the *Pont-du-roi*, a league and a half above *St. Béat*, it is known as the valley *d'Arran*, and forms a part of the province of *Catalonia*.

The valley of *Luchon*. This valley joins that of the *Garonne*, near the village of *Cierp*.

The valley of *Larboust*. This valley opens into the preceding, in the vicinity of *Bagneres de Luchon*.

The valley of *Louron*. The river of this valley flows into that of the valley *d'Aure*, near the town of *Arreau*.

The valley of *Aure*. This valley terminates among the low hills in the neighbourhood of *Barthe-de-Nestes*, and its river joins the *Garonne* near Montrejeau. The upper portion of this valley is called the valley of the *Neste*.

The valley of the *Campan*. This beautiful and much-famed valley has not its source in the central ridge, as all the others which I have mentioned, but is formed by a ramification of the great lateral chain which separates the valley *d'Aure* from that of the *Lavedan*. It opens into the plain near *Tarbes*, and its river, the *Adour*, flows into the bay of Biscay, near *Bayonne*.

The valley of *Héas*. This small, but very interesting valley, opens into that of the *Lavedan*, at the village of *Gèdre*.

The valley of the *Lavedan*. This great valley, although bearing the general name of the *Lavedan*, has nevertheless, in different districts, particular appellations. From its entrance to its source, under the walls of the Marboré, it bears the several names of the valley of *Argélèz*, of *Barèges*, and of *Gavarnie*, according as the portions of it are in the vicinity of one or other of these villages. It terminates at *Lourdes*, and its river, the Gave * of Pau, joins the Adour a few leagues from *Bayonne*.

* Throughout Bearn, and part of Bigorre, the word "gave" is a

The valley of *Cauteretz.* This valley is a tributary of that of the *Lavedan,* and unites with it near *Pierre-fittes.*

The valley of *Azun.* Another tributary of the *Lavedan,* opening into it near *Argélèz.*

The valley *d'Ossau.* This valley opens into the plain of *Arudy,* and its river, the *Gave of Oleron,* unites with that of *Pau* near *Peyhorade.*

The valley *d'Aspe.* This valley—famous as that through which the armies of France, in ancient times, on many occasions, passed into Spain—terminates among the hills near *Oleron,* and its river unites with the *Gave of Oleron.*

The valley of *Baretous.* This little valley terminates among the same hills as the preceding.

The valley of *Soule.* This valley, most frequently styled the *Pays de Soule,* terminates among the little hills in the vicinity of the town of Mauléon, and its river, the *Soisson,* unites with the *Gave of Oleron,* a short distance from *Sauveterre.*

The valley of *Cize.* This valley, sometimes called the *Pays de Cize,* unites with the valley of *Baigorry.*

The valley of *Louzaide.* This valley terminates in the basin of *Saint-Jean-Pied-de-Port,* formed by the

general term for all the rivers and torrents of the province; and to distinguish them, the name of the principal village or town which the river flows past, or valley through which it winds, is added.

valley of *Gize*. The upper part of this valley appertains to Spain.

The valley of *Baigorry*. This valley terminates below the watering-place of *Cambo*, and its river, the *Nive*, joins the *Adour* at Bayonne.

The valley of the *Bastan*. The greater part of this valley appertains to Spain, and the upper part of it is a portion of *Haute-Navarre*.

The valley of the *Bidassoa*. Nearly the whole of this valley is Spanish soil, forming part of the Biscayan province of *Guipuzcoa*.

Besides the above-mentioned valleys, there are a great number of others of inferior note, upon the northern side of the Pyreneés.

The principal valleys upon the southern or Spanish side of the Pyreneés, commencing upon the eastern extremity, are,

The valley of the *Muga*. The river of this valley flows past the town of *Figuerés*, in *Catalonia*, and into the gulf of *Rosas* in the *Mediterranean*.

The valley of the *Ter*. This valley is of much greater extent than the preceding. Its river, the *Ter*, flows past *Gironne*, and into the Mediterranean.

The valley of *Rigart*. This little valley opens into that of the *Ter*.

The valley of the *Sègre*. The upper part of this valley is the *French Cerdagne*. Its river, the *Sègre*, flows into the *Ebro*, near the fortress of *Mesquinensa*, in *Catalonia*.

The valley of *Balire*,

The valley of *Ordino*. These two valleys unite near the village of *Andorre*, and their rivers flow into the Sègre near the town of *Urgel*. These valleys, with their dependent lateral valleys and gorges, form the little republic of *Andorre*.

The valley of *Ferrara*,

The valley of *Cardous*. These two valleys unite near *Tirbia*, and their river flows into the *Noguera Paillaresa*.

The valley of *Paillas*. The river of this valley flows into the *Sègre*, near *Ballaguer*.

The valley of *Borri*. This valley is of small extent, and is watered by the *Noguera del Tort*, which flows into the *Noguera Ribagorsana*, near the village of *Torre*.

The valley of *Ribagorsana*. This valley is generally called the valley of *Senet*, and is beautiful as well as extensive. Its river joins the *Sègre* between *Ballaguer* and *Lerida*.

The valley of *Essera*. This valley is generally styled the valley of *Benasque*. Its river flows into the *Cinca*, between *Balbastro* and *Graus*.

The valley of *Gistain*. This valley unites with that of the *Cinca*, near the village of *Salinos*. The river which waters it is called the *Cinquetta*.

The valley of the *Cinca*. This valley is generally

called the valley of *Bielsa* or *Béouse*. Its river, the *Cinca*, has its source at the base of *Mont Perdu*, and it joins the *Sègre* a short distance before the latter unites with the *Ebro*.

The valley of *Brotto*. Its river, the *Arra*, flows into the *Cinca*, near the village of *Ainsa*.

The valley of *Thêne*. Its river, the *Gaillego*, flows into the *Ebro*, near *Sarragossa*.

The valley of *Canfrano*. This valley is watered by the *Aragon*, which at *Alfera*, falls into the *Ebro*.

The valley of *Asia*,
The valley of *Aragues*,
The valley of *Echo*,
The valley of *Anso*,
The valley of *Roncal*,
The valley of *Salazar*,
The valley of *Ahescoa*,
The valley of *Roncevaux*,
The valley of *Erro* :—

The waters of all these valleys flow into the *Aragon*.

The valley of *Heugui*, and that of *Lanz*, unite near *Pampeluna*, and their waters then flow into the *Ebro*.

Thus the whole of the waters which descend from the Spanish Pyreneés, with the exception of those of the *Muga*, the *Ter*, and the *Rigart*, flow into the Ebro. Those again on the French side, flow partly into the ocean and the Mediterranean, by various rivers.

Of the Glaciers in the Pyreneés those of

The *Maladetta*,
The *Crabioules*,
Mont Perdu,
The *Breche de Roland*,
The *Vignemale*, and
The *Neouvielle*, are the most considerable.

The Glacier of the *Maladetta* is situated in Spain, in the upper part of the valley of *Essera*, or *Benasque*, and a few leagues from *Bagnères de Luchon*.

The Glacier of the *Crabioules*, is situated at the head of the little valley of the *Lys*, which opens into that of *Luchon*. This Glacier unites with those of the *Portillon* and *Port d'Oo*.

The Glacier of *Mont Perdu*. This enormous mass of snow and ice is situated in Spain, at the source of the valley of the *Cinca*.

The Glacier of the *Breche de Roland*. This glacier is situated above the famous *Oule* of *Gavarnie*, at the source of the valley of the Lavedan. This glacier unites with that of the *Taillon*.

The Glacier of the *Vignemale*. This glacier is situated at the source of the little valley of *Ossonne*, one of the lateral valleys of the *Lavedan*. There are many inferior glaciers in its vicinity.

The Glacier of *Neouvielle*. This glacier, unlike the others, is at some distance from the central ridge, hanging upon one of the great mountains which separate the valley of the *Laredan* from that of *Aure*. It is very difficult to determine the region of perpetual snow, in the Pyreneés. Ramond has fixed it at 1350 or 1400 toises; but there are many mountains of much greater altitude, whose summits during a part of the season are void of snow.

The *Pic du Midi of Bigorre,* for instance, exceeds in height Ramond's region of perpetual snow, by at least 100 toises; and the snow leaves it in the month of August.

The climate of the two extremities of the Pyreneés, is much warmer than that of their central districts. Their proximity to the sea, their comparatively slight elevation above the level of the ocean, and their distance from the great mountains, are the principal cause of the great difference of temperature. The eastern extremity is again much warmer than the western, on account of its more southern situation. In *Roussillon,* we find the olive growing in luxuriance, and many other plants which are not to be met with in other parts of the Pyreneés.

With the exception of the high valleys, the climate is in general very mild in the districts bordering on the Pyreneés. The winter is very short, the cold by no means severe, and the snow which falls, very rarely remains beyond a day or two in the lower valleys. The summers are very warm; too warm for comfort, if the mountains were not near enough to fly to, and avoid them. Thunder-storms are very frequent in the summer, but are seldom of long duration, and are anxiously expected; as the rains which accompany them greatly cool the atmosphere.

In a climate such as that of the Pyreneés, vegetation cannot be otherwise than very fine, and accordingly we find the most abundant proof of it in all the Pyrenean valleys, whose fertility is perhaps unequalled in the world, and whose exquisite beauties are far too little known.

The Pyreneés abound in mineral springs, many of which have acquired a great celebrity from the cures which they are said to have effected. All the most frequented of the springs are under the superintendence of a physician, employed by the government, and great impartiality is observed in their administration. There is much necessity for this being the case, as often the demand for the waters is far above the supply.

The following are the most noted mineral springs in these mountains.

Bagnères de Bigorre. The period for taking these waters is from April to the end of October.

The springs are numerous, and there are about seventy baths. The most frequented are those of *Santè, Salut, Théas, Pré, Gultiere,* or *Cazeaux.* The others, which are warm springs, are: 1. *La Reine,* or spring of *Bagnerolles,* situated on a hill overlooking the town, and said to be the mother-spring; 2. *Le Dauphin;* 3. *La Nouvelle Fontaine,* belonging to Le Dauphin; 4. *St.*

Roch; 5. The two baths of *Foulon*; 6. *Le Petit Bain*, which is in the town; 7. *La Fontaine de Salies*; 8. *Le Petit Prieur*; 9. *Le Bain des Pauvres*; 10. La source d' Artique-*Longue*, now called the *Pinac* waters, after a physician who analyzed and made several interesting observations respecting them. The ferruginous spring of Angoulême rises on a hill to the south-west of Bagnères. The waters are diuretic, aperitive, and tonic, and are said to be efficacious in a great variety of disorders.

Bagnères de Luchon. The warm springs there have long been celebrated, and several Latin inscriptions attest that they were known to the Romans. The waters are taken from May to October; and there is an hospital for the poor. Some of the springs are warm, and others cold. They are called as follows: 1. *La Grotte*; 2. *La Salle*; 3. *Les Romaines*; 4. *Le Rocher*; 5. *La Reine*; this issues from the rock, and has been called by Campardon, the nursery of the waters of Luchon, as four other springs of different temperature rise near it; 6. *La Douce*; 7. *La Chaude à droite*; 8. *La Chaude à gauche*; 9, and 10. *Les Blanches*, separated by two other cold springs; 11 and 12, which are cold and slightly sulphureous.

These springs are situated at the foot of a mountain, near to each other, and are conducted beneath the ground into different reservoirs. The transparent waters look black, as the bottom of the reservoirs are lined with small slabs of slate; they emit a smell resembling musty eggs; their taste is flat; the action of the air, heat, and light, decomposes these waters, and gives them a milky appearance.

The medicinal properties of these waters bear considerable resemblance to those of Barèges and Cauteretz. They are employed both externally and internally, and are efficacious in chronic rheumatisms, paralysis, catarrh, and various other disorders. When drunk, they are taken pure, or mixed with milk.

Contiguous to the springs are sudatories, which are heated by the water which crosses them. These are but little frequented, and persons who go into them cannot remain more than a quarter of an hour, as the air is so hot and thick.

Barèges is celebrated for its mineral waters, which were known to Cæsar and Sertorius, who constructed buildings here worthy of Roman grandeur. Margaret, queen of Navarre, and sister of Francis I. visited these springs; and Henry IV. frequented them in his youth: Montaigne likewise visited them; and their fame was still further augmented by the residence of Madame de Maintenon, with the duke of Maine.

Barèges is annually visited by a great number of persons. The season lasts from May 20th to October 1st. Louis XV. erected a military hospital at Barèges, in which an immense number both of officers and soldiers have been healed.

There are three springs, the hot, the temperate, and the tepid, and five baths, three of which are close together. The names of the baths are: 1. *L'Entrée;* 2. The Great Basin, or Royal Bath; 3. *Le Fond;* 4. *Le Pollard;* 5. *La Chapelle;* or *La Grotte;* which is the highest as to situation. A pump is appropriated to the use of those drinking the waters, and there are two basins, each adapted for fourteen bathers. Although there are springs appropriated exclusively to the baths, the pump, and the douches, yet the waters are but slightly different.

The waters of Barèges are clear, but emit an unpleasant smell. They are particularly famous for healing wounds, and are also used in various disorders. They should be drunk on the spot, as carriage of course destroys their natural heat, and alters some of their properties. They are under the superintendence of a physician. In their effects they are generally aperitive, diuretic, and sudorific.

St. Sauveur. The bathing establishments consist of a douche, and fourteen other baths, which cannot, however, all be filled at the same time, on account of the small quantity of water furnished by the springs. The season commences in May, and ends in October. The lodgings here are commodious.

The mineral waters of St. Sauveur were not known in former times. According to tradition, a bishop of Tarbes, who was exiled at Luz, constructed, in the vicinity of the springs, a small chapel, with the following inscription: " Vos haurietis aquas de fontibus Salvatoris;" and from this inscription, it is said the place derived its name.

The principal spring is situated on a high mountain, from which the water is brought down to the baths by wooden pipes. There are two other springs on the heights.

The waters are taken inwardly for asthma, and obstructions of the viscera; and the baths are employed in rheumatic affections and contractions. The waters are milder than those of Barèges and Cauteretz, and are therefore more adapted to bilious and irritable temperaments.

Cauteretz. There are ten springs. A quarter of a league from this town, on the banks of the Gave, is the spring of *La Baillère,* where there is a saloon with four rooms.

Above the Baths of *Bruzault,* on the mountain towards the east, are the establishments of *Cæsar;* of *Les Espagnols,* also called *La Reine,* and *Pause,* very near each other, and difficult of access. There are also the springs of *Prè, Bois, Plaa, Manhourat,* and *Rieumiset,* or *des Yeux.*

The spring of Cæsar supplies the bottles which are

exported to all parts of France. The price of each bottle is 25 centimes; but visitors may drink at the springs gratuitously; and this is the case at all the springs in the arrondissement. The baths have been gradually improved, particularly at Manhourat and La Raillère.

The waters are efficacious in various cases, particularly in wounds, rheumatism, liver-complaints, intermittent fevers, consumption, ulcers, paralysis, and cutaneous disorders.

In the valley d'Ossau there are several springs of great celebrity; indeed those of the Eaux Bonnes are among the best known; and most frequented in the Pyreneés. They have three different sources; the first is styled *La Vielle;* the second, *La Source Neuve*, and the third, *La Source d'Ortech*. The first is the only one which is drunk, and its taste is any thing but agreeable to the palate.

The medicinal properties of these waters acquired great fame for them in ancient times, from the good effects which they wrought upon the Bearnais soldiers who had been wounded at Pavia. It was they who bestowed upon them the name of *Les Eaux d'Arquebusades*. Since those times they have acquired great reputation in curing pulmonary complaints, and individuals afflicted with these diseases, crowd to them from all parts of Europe.

In the adjacent valley, are the Eaux Chaudes, also well known at an early period, and still remarkable for the cures which they effect. Notwithstanding the frightful approach to these mineral springs, the little court of the kings of Navarre paid them an annual visit; and an inscription carved on the rock which overhangs the most dangerous pass, commemorates the occasion on which the Princess Catherine, sister of Henry IV., entered the wild and secluded valley.

There are five different sources of the Eaux Chaudes, almost all issuing from the granite. The first is called *La Houn deu Rerg;* the second, *L'Esquirette;* the third, *Le Trou;* the fourth, *L'Aresec,* and the fifth, *Main Vieille.* Their use is recommended in asthmatic complaints, and the baths for paralysis and rheumatisms.

On the road from Bagnères de Bigorre to Montrejeau, are the mineral springs of Capvern, whose baths, during the period of the Roman dominion in the South of France, were in great request; and now that the inhabitants of the village have erected handsome and comfortable accommodation for visitors, they are daily rising in importance. They are chiefly efficacious in chronic diseases.

In the valley of the Arriège, there are many mineral springs, and several beautifully situated watering-places.

The baths of Ussat, near Tarasçon, are much frequented. They are particularly efficacious in nervous affections, rheumatisms, and several other diseases.

In the same valley are the mineral springs of Ax, which have been considered of so much importance by the government, that an hospital has been built there for soldiers. They are very efficacious in asthmatic complaints and chronic affections, in paralysis, ulcers, &c.

In the valley of the Aude, is the beautiful little watering-place of Aleth. Its springs are efficacious in paralysis, in chronic affections, and diseases of the stomach.

In the valley of the Teta, is the charming little watering-place of Vernet, annually crowded with visitors from the south-eastern provinces of France, and the northern parts of Spain. They are chiefly useful as tonics.

In the same valley are the springs of Olette, of the same character as those of Ax. The springs of Las Escaldas in the same neighbourhood, are much the same as those of Barèges, Cauteretz, and the Eaux Bonnes. The baths of Las Escaldas have, from an early period, been much frequented.

In the valley of the Tet, are the mineral springs of Preste, near the Prats de Mollo; and those of Port les Bains, near Arles, the buildings of which last are supposed to have been constructed by the Romans. The springs of Preste have the same properties as those of Las Escaldas.

The waters of Arles are used as tonics, and are beneficial in rheumatisms, paralysis, and old musket-wounds.

There are many other mineral springs in the central and eastern departments of the Pyreneés, besides those already noticed, and some of them, such as those of Aulus and others, of considerable importance.

OF THE BEARNAIS LANGUAGE.

It was the author's intention to have inserted, along with the specimens of Bearnais Poetry, a glossary of the dialect: but the materials from which he would have drawn it up, not being at the present moment within his reach, he has not ventured from his own imperfect knowledge of the language, to supply it. The following illustration of the composition of the dialect may not, however, be deemed uninteresting.

Of the Verbs.

In the Bearnais dialect, the verbs—in which consists the true riches of a language—are very numerous. There are always many which express the same idea, at the same time modifying it; thus, besides the verb *brusla* (to burn), we find *cresma, creseca, ari ardé, eslama, ahouegna,* of which the force augments progressively.

Others may also be created at will from almost all the substantives; from *taule* (table) is formed *tauleya* (to sit at table); from *ardit* (a *liard*, a small piece of money) is formed *arditeya* (to collect a little money); from *pot* (to kiss) is formed *poutiqueya* (to give kisses), &c., &c.

Their conjugation is easy, regular, and graceful; the different moods are formed without the assistance of the pronouns, *I, thou, he,* &c., which gives a vivacity and rapidity of expression which is not to be found in the French language.

Of the Participles.

The participles are formed by adding to the infinitive the syllables *dou, dé,* or *dis,* in the masculine; *doure, dére,* or *disse* in the feminine. Thus *minya* (to eat), *minyadou, minyadoure,* who eats; minyadé, *minyadére* or *minyadis, minyadisse,* which may, or which ought to be eaten. *Ayma* (to love), *aymadou, amadoure,* who loves, *aymadé, aymadére,* or aymadis, *aymadisse,* who may, or who ought to be loved.

Reflective verbs are formed by the addition of the letter *s* to the termination of the infinitive, separated from it by an apostrophe, which takes the place of the (French) pronoun *se; birouleya* (to turn), *birouleya's* (to turn one's self).

Of the Substantives and the Adjectives.

The gender of the substantive is easily modified;

which permits of expressions being varied, and also allows of their being rendered more gentle or more strong, according to the circumstances; to effect this, nothing more is required than to make use of a diminutive, or of an augmentative, of which all the substantives are susceptible. Thus *la came* (the leg) is feminine; *la camotte, la camine* (the little leg), are also of the same gender; but *lou camot, lou camét, lou camou,* are of the masculine.

Those words of which the gender is not well determined, may even be changed without having recourse to diminutives or augmentatives; as in *gourg* or *gourgue* (a gathering together of water); *clot* or *clotte* (a ditch); *arram* or *arrame* (a branch); *bruc* or *bruque*, &c., &c.

Of Diminutives and Augmentatives.

Every substantive and adjective has its diminutive and its augmentative, which attaches to these words, at the will of him who employs them, agreeable or disagreeable ideas.

The diminutive is formed by adding to the end of the word the syllables *ett, ette,* to express joy, and pleasure; *in, ine,* to express friendship, tenderness, love; *ou, ot, otte,* to express pity or contempt.

The argumentative is formed by adding the syllables *as, asse;* it serves to express hatred, disdain, ridicule, or some disagreeable idea.

Thus from *hemne* (woman) is formed *hemnette* (little woman, agreeable to look at); *hemnine* (pretty little woman, whom one loves); *hemnou*, or hemnotte (poor little woman, whom one pities or despises); *hemnasse* (a gigantic woman; disagreeable; or whom one hates); *hemnassasse* is even sometimes said to augment the force of the expression.

Of the Vowels, and their Pronunciation.

The Bearnais dialect, like the Italian language, owes its sweetness to the great number of vowels which it contains; they form the *finales* of almost all words; their pronunciation is either long or short; soft or strong. The manner in which they are accentuated, indicates the different modulations, constituting that prosody, and that harmony, which renders the Bearnais the most poetic, as well as the most musical dialect of the south of France.

A and *o*, placed at the termination of words, have sometimes a feeble, sometimes a strong sound: those vowels which are strongly sounded, are distinguished by the *accent grave*, à, ò, sometimes even by doubling the vowel, as plàa (well), còo (heart).

O in the midst of a word is always short: but when placed at the end, it is almost always pronounced long; in this case, it stands for the French *e* mute, and is cut off in the same way as it; this last letter is even made use of in writing, giving it, however, the pronunciation of the *o*, by prolonging and softening the sound; thus the following words are written *amigue, berouyine, bouquette,* but they are pronounced *amiguo, berouyino, bouquetto.*

The *i*, like the *o*, may be sometimes long at the end of a word, but it is short elsewhere; thus it is short in *serbi* (to serve), *mouri* (to die), *mouli* (mill); and it is long in *cerbi* (stag), *que mouli* (I grind), *que'm mouri* (I die); in this last case, the *i* follows the same rules as the *ó*, that is to say, it is cut off in the same manner, and forms a feminine termination, whilst it is masculine when short.

In Bearnais, there are only two kinds of *e* known, the *é fermé* and the *è ouvert;* which are distinguished, the first by an accent *aigu*, and the second by an accent *grave*. As in these words *tendré* (tender), *tendrè* (tenderness), *abé* (to have), *abbè* (an abbé). But the *é fermé* has two different pronunciations; the one long, and the other short. It is long for example, in *bedé* (to see), *credé* (to believe), *redé* (stiff), *boulé* (to wish); and it is short in *abé* (to have), *sabé* (to know), *boulé* (the wish). Thus, as has been observed of the vowels *o* and *i*, the *é fermé* forms a masculine termination when it is short, and a feminine termination when long, and it is cut off in the same manner.

The *u* is also pronounced in two ways; like the French *u* in *madu* (a wall), *cadu* (each); and like the Italian *u* in the following words, *paü* (a stake), *seü*

APPENDIX. 291

(thirst), *ceü* (heaven), *arriü* (a brook), *poü* (fear); that is to say, as if they were *paou, seou, ceou, arriou, poou;* this last *u* is distinguished by ü.

The letter *h*, preceded by an *l*, takes the place of the French *ll mouillées*, either in the middle or at the end of a word, and is pronounced in the same manner. Thus *hilh* (son), *ailh* (garlic), *tourrouilh* (ice), *aülhette* (ewe), *aülhè*, are pronounced in this manner.

SPECIMENS OF BEARNAIS POETRY.

Roussignoulet cui cantes,
   Sus la branque paüsat,
Qu' èt plats, et que t' encantes,
   Aüprès de ta mieytat!
Et you plé de tristesse,
   Lou cô tout enclabat,
En quitan ma mestresse,
   Parti desesperat!

'Ere be pressentibe
   Lou die deü parti!
Lou cô que s'em mouribe
   De la béde souffri.
D'ûe bouts langourouse,
   Dits, m'estregnen la mâ:
"B èn seri malhurouse
   Sins calé sépara."

Youb' proumeti, la bère,
   D' eb ayma tendremen :
Ma paraüle ey sincère ;
   Ayat fé soulamen ;
Et siat assegurade,
   Que, louein d' aquets oueillous,
S' ére ma destinade,
   Souffriri mey que bous.

L' ayguette, la plus clare,
   L' arriü, lou plus poumpous,
De moun cô quis desglare,
   N' esgalen pas lous plous.
Nou-y-a carte, ni libe,
   D' û sort ta rigourous :
Arrés nou pot escribe
   Ni cantà mas doulous.

Taü coum la Tourterelle,
   En quitan soun pariou,
Moun cô toustem fidelle,
   Satineye à soun amou.
Oubyet de ma tendresse,
   Aü noum de l' amistat,
Plagnet lou quib adresse
   Soun darré adichat !

Moun doux amic s' en ba parti
　　S' en ba ta la Rouchelle;
Que herey you soulette acy
　　Oh! Milice cruelle!
Que herey you? quem baü mouri,
　　Louein de moun cô fidelle.

Beütat, esprit, lon me Pastou
　　Ben abé d' impourtance;
Bère taille et boune fayçou
　　Quoan se targabe en danse,
Et tà plà parla de l' amou
　　'N abé pariou en France.

En m' embrassan eth me digou,
　　Lous oueilhs tous plés de larmes:
Soubiente de toun serbidou
　　Qui ba pourta las armes,
En tà merita toun amou.
　　Diü las tristes allarmes!

Lou mati qui aü sort cadou;
  Eth me disé: "Beroye,
De serbi lou Rey moun Seignou
  Ben aüri la grand yoye
Si n' ére pas la toue doulou
  Qu' im hé mouri de roye."

Lou plus aymable deüs galans
  You l' ey pergut praübette,
Adichat flous, adiü ribans,
  Adiü douces flourettes;
You baü passa mouns plus bets ans
  Chens plasés amourettes.

Lous ciseüs que l' amic m' a dat
  Et la bague daürade
Dessus moun sé seran plaçats
  En aqueste journade,
De mouns plous seran arrousats
  Dinquò qu' em sic secade.

Gran Diü qui bedet moun turmen,
  Qué counechet ma peine,
Het—me rebede soulemen
  L' oubyet qui m' encadène;
Après, sat beye, prountamen;
  Het mouri Matalène.

Moun Diü quine souffrence,
    M' as-tu caüsat !
Dab quine indifférence
    M' as-tu quittat !
Quoan disés que m' aymabes
    Ta tendremen,
Labets tu qu' em troumpabes
    Crûelemen,
Et qu' êt félicitabes
    De moun tourmen !

Deüs qui tan fréquantade,
    Noun 'y a nat, nou,
Qui t' ayé tan aymade
    Coum hasi you.
Et per recounéchence,
    Bé m'as trahit !
Més moun maü dab l'absence
    Bé s' ey goârit ;
Yutye daquiü, et pense
    Ço qui m' an dit.

L' amou lou plus sincère
  Non t' ey d' arré :
Qu' aymes d' esta letiyére,
  Quey toun plazé ;
D' aütes s' y soun pecades,
  Chens pensa maü :
Que las an cayoulades
  Bet drin coum caü :
Après las an léchades,
  Ataü, ataü.

Mès you coum t' aymi hère,
  Bouy t' aberti,
Sin es à tems encouère,
  Abise-t' y :
U moumen de feblesso
  Pot arriba ;
Non seras pas mestresse
  De refusa ;
Ni mey per toun adresse,
  Deü répara.

Léche dounc, sim bos créde,
  Aquet garçou,
Qui souben té bien béde,
  Coum hasi you.

Pren garde à la glissade,
  Lou pas qu' ey dous ;
Sit lhébabes troumpade,
  Quines doulous !
Abise-t' y maynade :
  Gare lous plous !

Adichat, las mies amous,
    La bère Margalide :
En gouardan lous agnerous,
    Sib seret marfandide ?

—Non certes, moun amic dous,
    You moun soy marfandide :
Més l' ayguette de l' arrous,
    Que m' a drin refresquide.

Lou hâsà n' abé cantat,
    Que las mies oüillettes
You tirabi deü clédat,
    Per bous mas amourettes.

—You b' èri soü tucoulet
    A l' aübette deü die ;
Non-y-a que bous amiguet
    Qu' im desset facherie.

Lous montous de rouy pintrats,
 Lous trucs de las esquères,
Ben héran brut, s'a Diü plats
 Capbat las arribères.

—Biram, biram lou bestià,
 Per acéres endostes :
Tu qu' as burre, you qu' ey pà,
 Qu' ens heram senglés rostes.

Péchet, péchet, agnerous,
 Péchet, mas oüillettes.
En broustan aquestes flous,
 You qu' eb léchi soulettes.

—Et tu, petit Diü d' amous,
 Qui boles per lous aïres,
Ayes soueïn deüs amourous,
 Et lou troupet qu' em gouaytes.

—Adichat, dinqu' à douma ;
 Qu' em biret plâ l' aoüillade ;
Are, noum pouch mey triga ;
 Que seri trop cridade.

HEIGHTS OF THE MOST REMARKABLE PLACES IN THE PYRENEES.

A toise is about six feet four inches English measure.

	Toises.	Feet.
PERPIGNAN	10	63
CERET (bridge of), small town in the valley of the Tech	50	317
ARLES, a small town in the same valley	142	899
MONTFERET, village in the same valley	401	2539½
CANIGOU (mountain), between the valley of the Tech and that of the Teta	1442	9132½
MOSSET (mountain), between the valleys of the Teta and of the Aude, a little to the west of the Col de la Marguerite	1236	7828
ROC BLANC (mountain), at the head of the valley of the Aude	1302	8246
PIC PEYRIE, or PIC DE PRIGUE, at the head of the Gorge d'Orlu, between the valley of the Teta and that of Arriège	1427	9037½
PIC LANOUX, upon the ridge of the high chain, at		

	Toises.	Feet.
the head of the valley of Arriège............	1466	9284½
PIC PEDROUS, upon the ridge of the high chain, a short distance to the east of the Port de Puymorens at the head of the valley of the Arriége	1490	9433
PIC DE FONTARGENTE, on the ridge of the high chain, at the head of the little valley of Asson in the valley of the Arriège	1447	9164
PIC DE LA SERRERE, on the ridge of the high chain, at the head of the same little valley ...	1515	9595
PIC DU PORT DE SIGUIER, upon the ridge of the high chain, at the head of the little valley of Siguier	1504	9525
PORT DE RAT, at the head of the valley of Vicdessos	1169	7403½
MONTCALM, upon the ridge of the high chain, in the valley of Vicdessos	1660	10513
VICDESSOS	362	2292¼
PORT DE LHERZ, at the head of the little valley of Suc	778	4927
LAKE OF LHERZ	643	4072
SUC, village in the little valley of Suc	487	3084
SEM, village in the valley of Vicdessos	492	3116
ENTRANCE TO THE MINE OF RANCIE, called L'Auriette	641	4059½
ENTRANCE TO THE MINE OF RANCIE, called Crauque	700	4433
SUMMIT OF THE MOUNTAIN OF RANCIE	820	5193

APPENDIX. 303

	Toises.	Feet.
Pic, or Cap d'Endron, at the head of the little valley of Sem	1053	6729
Col de la Couillade, between the little valley of Suc and that of Gourbit	1016	6434½
Etang-Blau, small lake at the upper part of the little valley of Gourbit	921	5833
Prat d'Embans, valley of Gourbit	759	4807
Plateau de Cauties, in the same valley	486	3078
Pic de Saint Barthelemy, in the valley of Arriège	1190	7536½
Tarascon, valley of Arriège	237	1501
Foix, chief town of the department of Arriège	192	1216
Saint-Paul de Jarrat, valley of the Arriège	224	1418½
Pic de Mont Vallier, upon the ridge of the high chain, at the head of the valley of Sallat	1440	9120
Massat, town in the little valley of Soulan	303	1919
Saint-Girons, valley of the Sallat	211	1386
Angoumer, village in the valley of Castillon	232	1469
Maz d'Azil, little valley of Larize	135	855
Sainte-Croix, between this valley and that of the Sallat	126	798
Pic de Montouliou, or Tuc de Mauberme, upon the ridge of the high chain, at the head of the valley of Castillon	1488	9424
Mountain of Crabere, at the head of the little valley of Melles	1354	8575
Montarto, or Pic de Rious, upon the ridge of		

	Toises.	Feet.
the high chain to the south of Artiés, in the valleé d'Arran	1509	9557
PORT DE VIELLA, upon the ridge of the high chain	1286	8145
ETANG DU TORO	1034	6549
VIELLA, chief town of the valley d'Arran	452	2863
SAINT BEAT, in the valley of the Garonne	276	1748
PIC DE GAR, near Saint Béat	937	5934
BAGNERES DE LUCHON	314	1969
PORTILLON DE BURBE, between the valley of Luchon and that of Arran	644	4079
HOPITAL DE BAGNERES, at the foot of the Port de Venasque	696	4408
PORT DE LA PICADE, at the head of the valley of Luchon	1243	7872
PORT DE VENASQUE	1238	7841
LAKE OF THE PORT DE VENASQUE	1137	7201
PORT DE LA GLERE, to the west of the above mentioned	1192	7529
PRAT DE JOUO, in the little valley of the Port de la Glère	490	3103
CRABIOULES, upon the ridge of the high chain at the head of the valley de Lys	1650	10450
TUQUE DE MAUPAS, in the same valley	1615	10228
SUPERBAGNERES, mountain above Bagnères remarkable for its fine view	896	5675
MALADETTA (highest summit of), called the Pic d'Anethou	1787	11318

APPENDIX. 305

	Toises.	Feet.
Inaccessible ridge to the west of the Pic d'Anethou	1627	10304
Foot of the Glacier of the Maladetta (10th of September, 1811)	1371	8683
LAC D'ALBE	1135	7188
Edge of the Gouffre de Tourmon	1069	6770
Cabin at the PLAIN DES ETANGS, at the foot of the Maladetta	922	5839
Pic ar MAIL DE POUIS, or PIQUE FOURCANADE	1569	9937
HOPITAL DE VENASQUE	875	5542
TUQUE DE CIEYO, little valley of Astos of Benasque	1400	8867
PIC POSET, or LAS POSETS, opposite to the Port d'Oo upon the south side	1764	11172
PUNTA DE LARDANA, or PIC D'IRRE, between the valleys of Essera and of Gistain	1336	8461
PORT D'OO, at the head of the valley de Larboust	1540	9753
Frozen LAKE OF THE PORT D'OO	1361	8620
LAC D'ESPINGO, in the valley of Larboust	932	5903
Head of the CASCADE OF SECULEJO, in the valley of Larboust	878	5561
Lac de Seculéjo	718	4547
PLAINE D'ASTOS of Oo	564	3572
PIC QUAIRAT, between the valleys of Larboust and of Lys	1585	10038
PIC DE MONTAROUYE, a little to the north of the Pic Quairat	1438	9107
PIC DE HERMITANS, between the valleys of Lar-		

APPENDIX.

	Toises.	Feet.
boust and of Louron	1554	9842
PORT DE PEYRESOURDE, between the valleys of Larboust and of Louron	798	4991
LA SERRE DE SAINTE-PAUL, between the valley of Oueil and Luchon	962	6093
PORT DE LAPEZ, at the head of the valley of Louron	1265	8008
PIC DE BATOA, or BIEDOUS, between the Port of Lapez and that of Plan	1566	9918
PORT DE PLAN, at the head of the little valley of Rioumajou, in the valley of Aure	1151	7289
SERRE D'AZET, between the valley of Louron and that of Aure	804	5092
VILLAGE OF SAINT LARY, in the valley of Aure	400	2533
PIC D'ARRE (the higher), in the valley d'Aure	1504	9525
——————— (the lower)	1485	9405
PIC DÉ BAROUDE, upon the ridge of the high chain at the head of the valley d'Aure	1532	9703
PLAN D'ARRAGNOUET, last village of the valley d'Aure	684	4332
HOPITAL DE PLAN, in the valley of Gistain	768	4864
SANT-JEAN, chief town of the valley of Gistain	573	3629
Junction of the CINCETTE (torrent of the valley of Gistain) with the CINCA	392	2483
BIELSA, in the valley of the Cinca	514	3255
NOTRE-DAME DE PINEDE, at the head of the valley of the Cinca, and the nearest habitation		

	Toises.	Feet.
to Mont Perdu	667	4224
PORT VIEL, between the valley of the Cinca and that of Estaubé	1314	8322
PORT DE PINEDE	1291	8176
LAKE OF MONT PERDU, estimated at	1300	8233
COL DE NISCLE or of FANLO, opposite the Port de Pinéde	291	1843
MONT PERDU	1747	11264
CYLINDRE DU MARBORE	1729	10950
PIC DE LA CASCADE	1681	10646
TOUR DU MARBORE	1569	9933
BRECHE DE ROLAND	1542	9766
LE TAILLON, between the Breche de Roland and the Port de Gavarnie	1649	10443
PLAIN OF MILLARIS, upon the south side of the Marboré	1194	7562
ENTRANCE TO THE VALLEY OF ODESSA	556	3521
CIRQUE D'ESTAUBE, at the head of the valley of Estaubé	931	5896
BORNE DE TUQUE ROUYE, at the head of the same valley	1220	7727
BRECHE DE TUQUE ROUYE	1490	9417
COL DE PIMENE, or BRECHE D'ALLANS, between the valley of Zavadan and that of Estaubé	1291	8176
GRANGE DE GARGANTAN, at the entrance of the valley of Estaubé	902	5713
NOTRE DAME DE HÉAS, in the valley of Héas	740	4687

APPENDIX.

	Toises.	Feet.
Foot of the PORT DE LA CANAU and the CIRQUE DE TROUMOUSE	1060	6713
MOUNTAIN OF TROUMOUSE	1642	10399
PIC D'AIGUILLON, between the valley of Héas, and that of Aure	1523	9646
HOSPICE DE BOUCHARO, in the valley of Brotto	741	4693
PORT OF GAVARNIE, or of BOUCHARO	1172	7423
LAKE OF LOUBASSOU, at the upper part of the valley des Epessières	1131	7163
COMMENCEMENT OF THE CASCADE OF GAVARNIE	1166	10385
CIRQUE DE GAVARNIE, or HOULE DU MARBORÉ, at the foot of the cascade	985	6067
GAVARNIE (village of), in the valley of the Lavedan	735	4855
GEDRE (village of), in the valley of the Lavedan	546	3458
PIÇ DE CAMPBIEL, between the valley of Aure and that of Lavedan	1060	10513
PORT DE CAMPBIEL	1333	8442
PIC LONG, between the valley of Aure and that of Lavedan	1656	10488
PIC DE NEOUVIELLE, between the little valley of Couplan, and the valley of Bastan	1616	10235
PIC DE BERGONS	1108	7017
PIC D'EYRE	1267	8024
PIC D'ARBIZON, at the head of the valley of Campan	1460	9247
SAINT-SAUVEUR (baths of) in the valley of Lavedan	395	2502

	Toises.	Feet.
Luz (town of), in the same valley, at the entrance of the valley of Bastan	379	2400
Bareges, in the valley of the Bastan	658	4167
Col du Tourmalet, at the head of this valley	1126	7131
Pic du Midi de Bigorre	1493	9432
Pic de Montaigu	1192	7549
Penna de Lherys, in the valley of Campan	820	5193
Pierrefittes (village), in the valley of Lavedan	260	1647
Argelez	241	1526
Lourde, town at the entrance of the valley of the Lavedan	211	1336
Vignemale, at the head of the valley of Cauterez and of the little valley of Ossonne upon the ridge of the high chain	1721	10900
Pic de Badescure, at the head of the little valley of Bun	1615	10228
Pic d'Arrieugrand, at the extremity of the valley of Azun	1541	9760
Pic, or Som de Soube	1607	10178
Pic du Midi d'Ossau	1531	9696
Pic d'Aule, to the north-west of the Pic du Midi d'Ossau	1505	9532
Pic d'Anie, upon the ridge of the high chain between the valley d'Aspe and that of Soule	1326	8398
Mountain of Orhi, upon the ridge of the high chain at the head of the valley of Soule	1031	6530
Orsan-Sourrietta (mountain of)	801	5073

	Toises.	Feet.
MOUNTAIN OF HAUSA, between the valley of Baigorry and that of Bastan	667	4224
MOUNTAIN OF HAYA, or of QUATRE-COURONNES in the Guipuzcoa	500	3167
MOUNTAIN OF AISQUIBEL, upon the sea-coast, between Bidassoa and the Port du Passage	278	1761
TARBES	150	950
TOULOUSE (Place Royale)	73	462

APPENDIX.

EXPLANATION OF CERTAIN TERMS PECULIAR TO THE PYRENEES.

Cacou—The most simply constructed cabin of the shepherds.

Chaos—confused heaps of immense rocks.

Cirque—the circular basin inclosed by vast precipices, found at the source of many valleys.

Core—small *Port* or passage.

Couïla—Cabin of the shepherds of the Hautes Pyreneés.

Couret—the course of a river when it leaves a lake.

Courtaou—Cabin of the shepherds of the Couserans.

Estibe—Fine meadows.

Gave—Generic name for rivers in Bigorre and Bearn.

Hourque, Hourquette—A little port or passage in Bigorre.

Mail—Mountain in the valleys of the Garonne.

Neste—Generic name for rivers in Bigorre.
Oule—Local name for the *Cirques*.
Orris—Shepherds' cabin in the county of Foix.
Pene—The extreme point of a mountain.
Pouey, Puch, Pech, Puy, &c.—Mountain.
Raillere—Space covered with fragments of fallen rock.
Ramade—Great flocks.
Roule—The trunk of a tree meant to be sawed.
Sarre, Serre, Serrat—Mountain.
Seoube—Forest.
Tuc, Tuque—Mountain.
Turon—Little hillock.

END OF VOL. II.